THE *Blu*

CRICKET

James Trollope and Nick Yapp

Bluffer's®

Colette House
52-55 Piccadilly
London W1J 0DX
United Kingdom

Email: info@bluffers.com
Website: bluffers.com
Twitter: @BluffersGuide

First published 1988
This edition published 2013

Publisher: Thomas Drewry
Publishing Director: Brooke McDonald

Series Editor: David Allsop
Design and Illustration by Jim Shannon

A CIP Catalogue record for this book is available from the British Library.

ISBN: 978-1-909365-12-4 (print)
978-1-909365-13-1 (ePub)
978-1-909365-14-8 (Kindle)

CONTENTS

It has been said that the English, not being by nature a religious people, invented cricket to give them some idea of Eternity.

PRE-MATCH DRILL

It has been said that the English, not being by nature a religious people, invented cricket to give them some idea of Eternity. This is blatant bluffing, though it does indicate that cricket is not to be treated lightly or dismissed as merely a sport. The English did not invent cricket, but they acted as its wet nurse, nurtured it, and finally made it their own. This is because cricket needs endless patience, unthinking loyalty and a slavish mentality: not the sort of game you can see being enjoyed by the hordes of Genghis Khan, the Sioux, the Paris mob of 1789 or the Bolsheviks.

GM Trevelyan – famous historian and useful late-order bat – once suggested that, if the aristocracy of the Ancien Régime had spent more time playing cricket with their serfs, the French Revolution would never have taken place. The truth is that neither the French aristocracy nor their serfs could ever have wanted to play cricket; it is not their game.

Bored almost beyond endurance, the uninitiated spectators and even players of cricket will moan: 'What's the point of it?' Bluffers know that there is no point to cricket, any more than there is a point to tennis, ballet, rose gardens or *nouvelle cuisine*.

Cricket maintains its precarious existence because 'the show must go on.' It has to be demonstrated that people can:

- Bowl faster.
- Score more runs.
- Make more appearances for their county.
- Take longer to score a run than ever before.

This, you must maintain stoutly (cricketers do lots of things stoutly), provides proof of human progress.

Support for English cricket – the distinguished variety which is the main focus of this guide – fluctuates with the performance of the national team. During decades of defeat, first by the West Indians and then the Australians, and then everybody else, it was reduced to a hardcore of thermos-gripping fans scattered thinly across increasingly shabby county grounds. But then, as the England team did better, interest revived. Smart new stands went up, new technology was introduced and a shorter form of the game called Twenty20 began pulling in large crowds. Now, it seems, cricket is in danger of becoming sexy – and that's not a bluff.

Winning the Ashes in 2005, after 18 miserable, soul-searching years, was a vital turning point for England (more on the history of this venerable contest later). Fair-weather supporters suddenly appeared in droves, with politicians and other inveterate bluffers suggesting that they'd been lifelong fans all along. A few even hinted that, in their time, they'd been more than useful players themselves. When it was reported that, during an extended post-victory bender, Ashes hero Andrew 'Freddie' Flintoff had relieved himself in the prime minister's rose garden, even some of the stuffiest cricket followers found it easy to smile indulgently.

To listeners of the BBC's *Test Match Special*, another boundary was crossed in 2009 when sassy young pop star Lily Allen (now known as Lily Rose Cooper) told presenter Jonathan Agnew (Aggers) that she'd taken a fancy to the game and to fast bowler Graham Onions in particular.

Lily also showed an unexpected depth of cricket knowledge when she revealed that she preferred Tests to Twenty20 and old-fashioned cream flannels to the dazzling whites worn by the England team (who, despite this fashion blunder, managed to beat the Australians again that same summer). England and Lily (then tweeting about cricket to a million-plus followers) were on a roll.

In a second commentary box chat two years later, the same fragrant singer told Aggers how she was on the list to join the MCC (Marylebone Cricket Club – waiting time for membership about 18 years) and how, more pressingly, she was about to make tea for husband Sam's village team in Gloucestershire. For some reason she clearly didn't foresee much of a future as Mrs Onions.

By 2011, when England topped the world rankings, having thrashed the Aussies in their own backyard, an ignorance of cricket had become a social handicap, carrying with it risk of exclusion from pub, party and office chat. To the rescue comes a new, updated, equally authoritative *Bluffer's Guide.*

Cricket bluffing ranges from hinting that you know more than you do, which is the general idea, to extravagant claims of a dazzling cricketing past, which is somewhat riskier. An extreme bluffer may even take the dangerous step of accepting an invitation to play. This is not recommended.

Before you start bluffing, a word of warning. Size up your victim. Try to sound out how much, if anything, they know. Take particular care at a cricket ground. If they are wearing a lurid 'egg-and-bacon'-coloured blazer – the preferred uniform of members of the MCC, which effectively runs the game – or walk with pigeon feet (sign of a pace bowler), proceed with caution. If they are carrying a copy of the cricket annual *Wisden* or, worse still, a scorebook, run a mile.

This short but definitive guide will conduct you through the main danger zones often encountered in discussions about cricket. It will equip you with a vocabulary, easy-to-learn hints and evasive technique that will minimise the risk of being rumbled as a bluffer – and might even allow you to be accepted as a cricketing connoisseur of rare ability and experience. But it will do more. It will give you the tools to impress legions of marvelling listeners with your knowledge and insight – without anyone discovering that, until you read it, you didn't actually know the difference between bowling a maiden over and bagging a pair.

PLAY!

Tiresome though it might seem, only a fool will start bluffing without a basic knowledge of how to play the game. Don't worry too much about the finer points; some professionals have only a slender grasp. Instead, top up any memories of childhood cricket with doses of the televised stuff and you'll soon be halfway there. The TV coverage will probably take you back to the playground anyway as much of it is dominated by overgrown schoolboys with nicknames like Beefy and Bumble. But despite the larking about, these chaps know their cricket. You may remember that Sir Ian 'Beefy' Botham had one or two useful games for England, while Bumble (David Lloyd) was not only a top-class batsman but a coach and umpire, too. You will need to be familiar with these names (and nicknames) if you are to withstand close scrutiny in the company of genuine cricket aficionados.

The rudiments of cricket are the same whether played by keen amateurs on a village green or seasoned professionals in a packed stadium. Two sides of 11 players 'bat' or 'field'. The batsmen (or 'batters' if you prefer to be non-gender-specific) try to make as many runs as possible while the bowlers and fielders try to get them out for as few runs as possible. Getting a batsman out is known as a 'wicket'.

Cricket is all about scoring runs and taking wickets (and statistics, of which more later). In most matches, the side that scores the greater number of runs wins. Perhaps the simplest way to explain the game is to describe what happens from the beginning:

1. A field is mown. A 'square' in the middle is mown even shorter. A 'pitch' on the square is mown shortest of all, so that there isn't any grass left.

2. Two white 'creases' are painted at each end of the pitch. They mark the areas from which a bowler may safely bowl and in which a batsman may safely stand.

3. Three sticks, called 'stumps', are tapped into the ground at each end of the pitch.

4. Two people wearing white coats enter the cricket field. They are not psychiatrists, but perhaps they should be. They place little bridging pieces of wood, called 'bails', on both sets of stumps. They are known as 'umpires'.

5. The umpires spend a lot of time inspecting the match cricket ball and looking at the glowering sky.

(All this activity, and the game hasn't even started yet.)

6. The fielding side come out of the pavilion, exuding confidence and barely contained pent-up aggression.

The captain leads, followed by minor members of the aristocracy, ordained ministers, visiting politicians and, last of all, sweaty but honest professionals.

7. Two batsmen emerge, pale but proud. The 'non-striker' stands by the bowler's wicket. The 'striker' stands by the other wicket.

8. One umpire throws the ball to the bowler and shouts 'Play!'.

9. It starts to rain. The bowler runs up and hurls the ball at the striker, or the wicket, or somewhere roughly in that direction.

10. After six such hurls (an 'over') the bowling switches to the other end and somebody else has a go.

From this point onwards, it is a matter of the batsmen getting as many runs as possible, and the bowlers and fielders getting them out.

A run is scored when one batsman swipes the ball with his bat, and the two batsmen 'cross' in the middle of the 'pitch' (also known as the 'wicket') and regain the safety of their crease (*see* next page for 'Boundaries'). A team can win, lose or tie. When a game runs out of time, it's called a 'draw'. Other less knowledgeable observers might refer to this as a 'waste of time'. They would be wrong, because a draw can be as gripping a spectacle as a match with a conclusive result. It is impossible to explain this to many non-English-speaking people (particularly Americans), but state it with confidence, because it is undeniably true. A draw snatched from the jaws of defeat can sometimes be more satisfying than a win – even after five interminable days' play.

MAKING RUNS

Runs can either be scored by the batsman hitting the ball with his bat or by a method called 'extras'.

There are two ways that a batsman can score runs with the bat:

1. The batsman hits the ball out of the field of play (six runs without bouncing, four runs with). This is called a 'boundary' and spectators are expected to wake up and clap. The batsmen do not have to run, but generally meet in the middle of the wicket to 'punch' gloves and gloat about scoring without having to waste energy running up and down the wicket.

2. The batsman hits the ball far enough for both batsmen to change ends. This can be exciting, since each has to judge the safety of his or her position. It often leads to the following sort of verbal exchange:

   Striker Yes!

   Non-striker Wait!

   Striker (***who will be credited with the run if they make it***) Come on!

   Non-striker No!!

   Striker (***now several strides down the wicket***) Run, you fool!

Non-striker (*damned if he or she is risking being out for another batsman's run*) Get back!

Striker (*damned if he or she is going back*) Come ON!!

Non-striker **** off!!

By now, both batsmen are at the same end of the pitch, looking at each other with barely disguised loathing. At the other end, the fielding side have removed the bails with the now-returned ball and are covering their mouths to stifle their sniggers. One of the batsmen is out. Which? Probably the non-striker, the more passive of the two, although the Laws of Cricket would say otherwise. Either way, one batsman has to make the supreme sacrifice and walk back to the pavilion like a white-flannelled Sydney Carton. Vast sympathy awaits.

Cricket is flooded with sympathy... The more inept the performance, the greater the sympathy.

Cricket is flooded with sympathy. Sympathy for being out; for having been given out when you weren't; for letting the ball pass between your feet and looking foolish; for bowling all afternoon and not taking a single wicket; for not getting a chance to bowl; for bowling a load of tripe and being hit all over the park; for scoring no runs; for scoring 99 runs; for not getting a chance to bat; for dropping eight simple catches. The more inept the performance, the greater the sympathy.

The batting team can also be awarded runs by way of extras. These consist of:

Bye The batsman misses the ball; so does the wicketkeeper (the fielder immediately behind the stumps wearing huge padded gloves). Everyone looks foolish. The batsmen change ends.

Leg bye The ball, not in line with the wicket (otherwise leg before wicket or 'lbw'), hits the batsman's leg or body. It bounces far enough away for the batsmen to change ends.

No-ball The bowler oversteps the crease while delivering the ball. The umpire is supposed to shout 'N' ba'!' and to stick an arm out sideways (trying not to decapitate the bowler) so the batsman knows he may take a mighty swing at the ball, since the only way you can be out off a no-ball is to be 'run out' (*see* Ways of Getting Out, below).

Wide The ball is bowled so wide of the wicket that a batsman could not be reasonably expected to hit it, even if he were nimble enough to get close.

WAYS OF GETTING OUT

There are many ways to get 'out':

Bowled The batsman hits or misses the ball, which travels on and knocks a bail off the stumps. Or the ball uproots the stumps from the ground, which amounts to the same thing (except that it is much more humiliating for the batsman).

Caught The batsman hits the ball, which is grabbed by the fielder or bowler before it hits the ground.

Stumped The batsman misses the ball and has foolishly left 'safe' ground in his attempt to bludgeon it to the far corners of the ground. The wicketkeeper catches the ball. The batsman is still out of his crease. The wicketkeeper removes a bail by striking the stumps with the hand in which the ball is held.

Run-out The batsman hits or misses the ball and tries to run from one end of the pitch to the other, or leaves the crease and tries to get back. But before regaining safe ground, the fielder either throws the ball to the bowler or wicketkeeper (who do as in stumped) or throws the ball directly on to the wicket, knocking a bail off.

Hit wicket While trying to hit the ball, the batsman hits his own wicket. The *hara-kiri* of cricket.

Leg before wicket (lbw) Diabolically hard to understand, but involving the ball hitting the batsman's leg when it would otherwise have hit the wicket. This is not always the case, however. Rather like the offside rule in football, nobody is quite sure how it works.

There are three other ways to be 'out': **handled the ball, hit the ball twice** and **obstructed the field.** It should be clear from their titles what they entail, and that they apply only to absolute bounders. Some bowlers believe that the best way to dismiss a batsman is by crippling him (*see* 'The Bodyline Tour', page 27). Since there must be two batsmen available at any time, a complete side of 11 is dismissed when 10 wickets have fallen or 10 batsmen have been crippled.

APPEALS

Sometimes it is obvious when a batsman is dismissed. The stumps may be spreadeagled as previously described or the ball clearly caught. Also, the batsman's upper lip stiffens while the lower one quivers. But often there is room for doubt. It is here that the 'appeal' comes into play. In theory, one from the fielding side has to enquire politely, 'How was that?', and the umpire has to respond either by indicating that the batsman is out or by saying that he isn't.

In practice, the bowler and as many fielders as are still awake scream a monosyllabic 'Zzhhaarrtt!', and the umpire either indicates 'out' or snorts contemptuously. It is not unknown for modern cricketers to disagree with the umpire and display a degree of anguish if their appeal is disallowed. This display may take the form of spitting, punching the ground, twisting the features of the face into an ugly pattern or, apparently, mouthing the words 'flipping heck!'.

FIELDING POSITIONS

Never call anyone a 'backstop'. There is no such position in cricket, and it shows you to be a complete duffer, not bluffer, fit only for softball or rounders. There is, however, a 'longstop' but this position is only occupied when the fielding side has an appallingly bad wicketkeeper. Since it is considered a disgrace to need a longstop, put someone in the longstop position only when strictly necessary but call them 'very fine leg'.

Sadly, there are not enough fielders to go everywhere the ball is most likely to be hit, so the captain, in consultation with the bowler and the team's nosy parker, decides which nine gaps he will attempt to plug. At the beginning of an innings, when one side goes 'in' and when the bowler has a bright, shiny, hard new ball and the batsmen are unsure and haven't 'got their eyes in', the captain will set what is called an 'attacking' field. This means that most of the fielders are behind the batsman, looking menacingly at the bowler.

Once the shine has gone from the ball and the batsmen are well set and the bowlers tired, the captain will set a 'defensive' field. This means that all the fielders are behind the bowler, looking menacingly at the batsman.

You can generally put your fielders where you like, but there are some rules and restrictions. Fast bowlers like to put all their fielders near the batsman. This is because fast bowlers rely on brute strength and do not expect a batsman to do more than defend. Slow bowlers like to put all their fielders as far away from the batsman as possible. This is because slow bowlers rely on guile and cunning and expect that the batsman will thrash his/her bowling all over the place. There is probably a deep truth about the human condition here. There are deep truths about the human condition throughout cricket.

Bluffers should be wary of cricketing clichés such as 'Cricket is a funny old game' or 'It's fielders who win matches'. In school or club cricket, the latter is meant to stiffen the

Bluffers should be wary of cricketing clichés such as, 'Cricket is a funny old game' or, 'It's fielders who win matches'.

resolve of those who are rotten batsmen or bowlers and who are only in the team to make up the numbers. But at county or international level it approaches the truth. One dropped catch can cost a match; one brilliant 'run out' may save a match. Some of the greatest sights in cricket are those of really good fielders racing across the grass, swooping to pick up the ball on the run, then throwing it to the wicketkeeper with the speed and accuracy of a well-aimed bullet. It only looks awful if it goes wrong.

In the old days, fielding was regarded as a chore. Batting and bowling were what mattered. You didn't get your name in the paper for running after a ball that someone else had hit off someone else's bowling. 'Lithe', 'supple' and 'lissom' were not words generally applied to WG Grace, Alfred Mynn or 'Lumpy' Stevens. Only 50 years ago, it was regular practice to stick out a large boot to stop the ball and only the eccentric or show-offs would dive, even for a catch. Nowadays, fielders are expected to throw themselves upwards, downwards and sideways, even if it means permanent physical damage. A lot of cricket coaching focuses on overriding natural self-preservation instincts.

ATTACKING FIELD

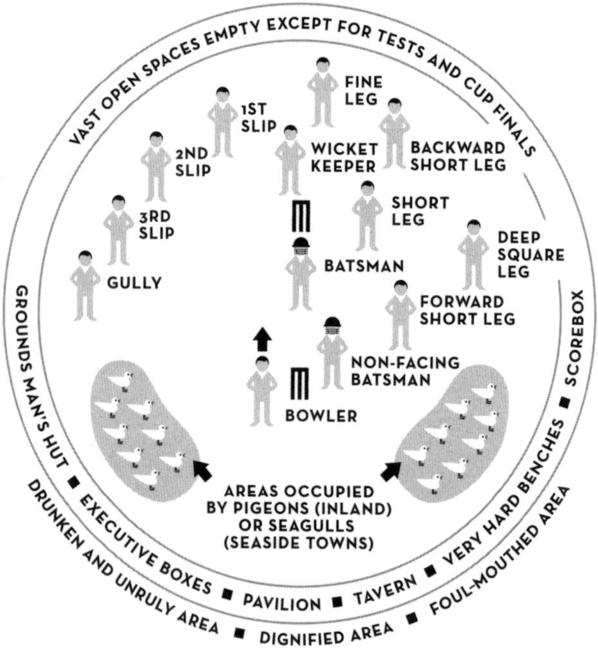

DEFENSIVE FIELD

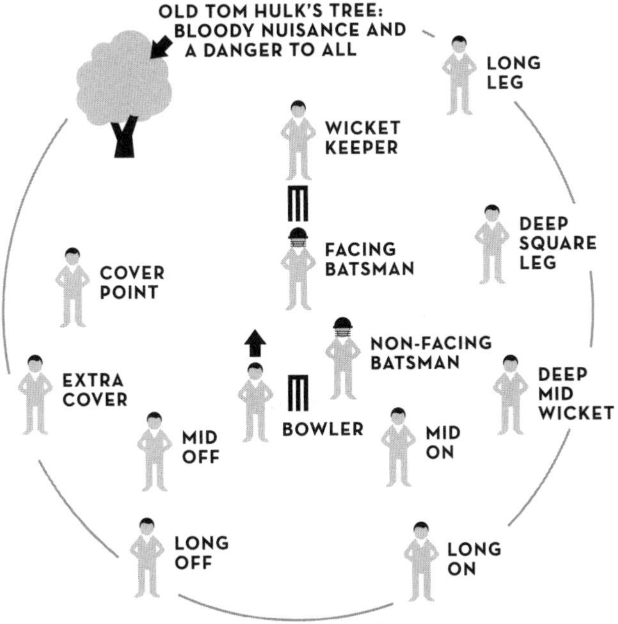
OLD TOM HULK'S TREE:
BLOODY NUISANCE AND
A DANGER TO ALL
LONG
LEG
WICKET
KEEPER
DEEP
SQUARE
LEG
FACING
BATSMAN
COVER
POINT
NON-FACING
BATSMAN
EXTRA
COVER
DEEP
MID
WICKET
MID
OFF
BOWLER
MID
ON
LONG
OFF
LONG
ON

In August 1882, in a match that lasted only two days, Australia beat England for the first time in England. One spectator dropped dead and another bit chunks out of his umbrella handle.

EVOLUTION OF THE GAME

While many potential bluffers won't want to get too bogged down in the history of cricket, it's as well to have some idea about its origins, development and organisation. (For those of a more studious bent who feel safer bluffing about the past, there's more in a later chapter.)

At the top level of the English game, the overriding aim is to humiliate the Australians. But below that, there are many ways to get involved – as a spectator, player, umpire, scorer and, of course, bluffer.

ORIGINS

No one even knows the origin of the word 'cricket', let alone the game, but it seems to be derived from either the Anglo-Saxon *cricce*, the French *criquet* or the Dutch *krickstoel.*

A *cricce* was a staff or crutch. In the University of Oxford's Bodleian Library, there is a picture of medieval monks standing in a field, one brother bowling a spherical object to another who is attempting to hit it with his *cricce* (difficult when you're wearing a heavy woollen frock). Instead of a wicket there is a hole in the ground. This is reckoned by experts to be a very early form of the game 'club-ball', cricket's forerunner. But it could simply be a picture of some medieval monks being silly in a field.

There are references in fifteenth-century French literature to *criquet* (it was played at St Omer as soon as they'd got over the Hundred Years War) and in a sixteenth-century Italian dictionary to *cricket-a-wicket*. This cosmopolitan scattering of information is perfect for bluffing purposes. You can wax lyrical over why it never caught on in Italy – imagine fielding at cover after a *torta milanesa* – and speculate wildly about the game's simultaneous development in Denmark, Holland, Germany and Persia (where it was called *kruitskaukan*). There is probably a picture in Tehran University of a group of ayatollahs being silly in a field (possibly also wearing frocks).

In 1617 Oliver Cromwell is said to have thrown himself into a 'dissolute and disorderly course' by playing cricket; there's depravity for you. In 1676 a party of British sailors played cricket in Aleppo. This does not explain what they were doing in Syria, some 80 miles inland, when they were supposed to have been fighting the Dutch in the Medway, but it may be evidence of cricket's early international prestige.

THE MARYLEBONE CRICKET CLUB

The headquarters of the MCC are at Lord's in a posh part of London called St John's Wood. It was founded in 1787 by ex-patrons of the Hambledon Club, which up to then had regarded itself as the controller of the game. As Lily Rose Cooper will tell you, it's considered something of an honour to become a member, although not so notable a distinction as being kicked out. This has only been achieved publicly in recent times by that champion bluffer Jeffrey Archer, who was suspended for seven years after being convicted of perjury. After a spell behind bars, he's now back in the venerable club which pronounces on the rights and wrongs of the game. Other members of the MCC include such stalwarts of the establishment as Sir Mick Jagger, shortly to be joined by the future Dame Lily (it's only a matter of time). There is a waiting list of several thousand, and, if you are a man, you will have to show that you wear a suit, collar and tie at all times, treat women like ladies, know your way round a decent wine list and are able to sleep on a hard seat in the open air.

The MCC is the custodian of cricket. It has a museum of the game, a collection of books, more memorabilia than it has room for, and is the self-appointed guardian of the game of cricket. Because it is based in London, it is viewed with great suspicion by all the county clubs except Middlesex, who share Lord's with the MCC and are consequently given preferential treatment. The bright bluffer knows that this is why Middlesex play all their cup finals on their home ground, and why there have been more captains of England from Middlesex than any other county.

THE ASHES

The Ashes is a 'Test' series that takes place every two years between England and Australia, alternately in each country. Most followers of English and Australian cricket say that it should be played every year, because it is the only one they really care about.

In August 1882, in a match that lasted only two days, Australia beat England for the first time in England. One spectator dropped dead and another bit chunks out of his umbrella handle (Augusts were soaking wet 100 years ago too). The next day, *The Sporting Times* published its famous mock obituary:

> *In affectionate Remembrance of English Cricket which died at the Oval on 29th August, 1882. Deeply lamented by a large circle of sorrowing friends and acquaintances. RIP. NB The body will be cremated and the ashes taken to Australia.*

The following winter, England beat Australia in Australia, and some Melbourne ladies burnt a bail, sealed the ashes in an urn and inscribed it with a rather sweet little poem that included the couplet: 'The welkin will ring loud/The great crowd will feel proud.' Australians have always been better at cricket than poetry.

The ladies presented the urn to the English captain, the Honourable Ivo Bligh, and one of them subsequently married him. When the Hon Ivo died, he bequeathed the Ashes to the MCC.

Since 1927 they have remained at Lord's, even though England did not win them once from 1934 until 1953.

THE BODYLINE TOUR

Once upon a time it was all very different. The Ashes mattered enormously to everyone. National pride was at stake.

In 1930, Australia beat England in England. Normally, a gunboat would have been dispatched to shell Sydney Harbour but, instead, in the winter of 1932-1933, Douglas Jardine was sent to Australia with a team that included three lethally fast bowlers: Harold Larwood, Bill Voce and Bill Bowes. Everyone roughly agrees on what happened next, but there are different versions as to how it happened and why it happened.

The *Boy's Own Paper* theory suggests that Jardine was a jolly good public school-educated chap who understandably found it hard to talk to the colonials when they squealed about being hit on the head and heart by a hard ball propelled at speeds in excess of 90mph.

The Establishment theory is that the whole thing was badly handled, and would have been sorted out in 10 seconds pronto by the autocratic Lord Harris of Seringapatam, Mysore and Belmont (who must have been a pretty smart fellow, being Lord of places so far apart) if this former England captain and MCC president had not been so careless as to die the previous spring.

The professional cricketers' theory is that they had to do as they were told by the amateur captain.

The modern sports psychologist's theory is that motivation to win should peak some time before homicidal intent sets in.

The Oz School of Journalism theory suggests that the whingeing poms were so scared of Don Bradman, who had averaged around 150 runs per innings in the 1930 Test series, that the English bowlers resorted to Australian methods of removing him – which just wasn't cricket.

Bodyline theory was very simple. You just placed a cordon of fielders near the wicket on the leg side (*see* 'Glossary', page 112) and bowled at the batsman's body.

The Australians were incensed. Their Board of Control sent an alarmist cable to the MCC. The MCC Committee met to discuss it. At that time, the Committee consisted of:

Six peers
Five knights
The speaker of the House of Commons
The chairman of the Unionist Party
An ex-governor of Bengal
A cabinet minister
A Lord Mayor of London
Six cricketers (No one is quite sure why they were there).

So the Committee clearly had its ear to the ground, knew what the man on the street was thinking, finger on the pulse of democracy, etc. More cables were sent. A couple of England players were disciplined. The Australian crowds were condemned for dishing out verbal abuse at the matches where their players were injured. More significantly, the laws were modified to outlaw bodyline bowling.

Today, umpires are empowered to warn a bowler if they think he is deliberately intimidating a batsman. If the bowler does not heed the warning, the umpires can warn him/her again. And again. And then a few more times before instructing the captain that he/she may bowl no more in that innings. And restrictions were placed on the number of fielders you could put close to the wicket on the leg side.

Australia is still a member of the Commonwealth (just).

THE LAWS OF CRICKET

The present laws of cricket are still roughly those laid down by Sir William Draper, His Grace the Duke of Dorset and some of their boozy chums one night in February 1774. There are 42 laws in all, many with several clauses and sub-clauses. They cover substitutes; time-wasting; umpires; the rolling, sweeping, mowing, watering and marking of the pitch; the tea interval; dead balls; and unfair play, which includes 'lifting the seam', 'incommoding the striker' and unfairly 'stealing a run'. They are very soberly written, much venerated and occupy more than 30 pages of very small print.

Cricket has laws, not rules. There is, however, no system of appeal to the House of Lords, far less to the European Court of Human Rights. You have to rely on the umpires.

UMPIRES

If you have been captivating an audience about your cricketing prowess in the local pub, you might find yourself asked to step in to officiate the following day. This is actually worse than being asked to play, because you'll be expected to have some understanding of the game. The following brief exposition of an umpire's duties might therefore help:

1. Make sure that play starts on time.
2. Make sure that the fielding side does not cheat by having too many people in their team or by placing them illegally in the field.
3. Shout 'Play!' so that a match can begin.
4. Count up to six and then shout 'Over!'.
5. Make sure that the bowler does not bowl a no-ball.
6. Hold the bowler's sweater and cap while he or she bowls.
7. Make sure that the batsman covers the full length of the pitch for a run.
8. Signal byes, wides, boundaries, etc. to the scorers.
9. Check that the light is good enough.
10. Make sure that each session of play ends promptly.
11. Adjudicate whenever a bowler and/or fielders appeal for a catch, stumping, lbw, run out and so forth.

There is also someone known as a 'third umpire' but this really only applies at the professional level. Nonetheless you should be acquainted with his job, which is to sit in a warm room in the pavilion, watch TV and snooze. When there is an appeal for a run out, the third umpire is awakened and his attention is directed to a video replay of what happened. He then decides the outcome of the appeal before going back to sleep.

In county and Test cricket, the umpire's role calls for fine judgment and complete impartiality, together with the ability to appease a volatile and partisan crowd. In the past, they tended to be cuddly or wizened veterans but now, perhaps fresh from a recent playing career, they're often disconcertingly youthful. They inform a batsman that he is out by raising the index finger of the right hand and, like a police officer controlling traffic, have a variety of other signals.

As TV coverage of the game has spread, international umpires have been put increasingly in the spotlight. Most

There is a feeling that if you shout loud enough, often enough, the umpire will have to submit, sooner or later.

have reacted with appropriate modesty but a few have become irritatingly attention-seeking. The behaviour of the legitimate celebrities of the game (the players) has remained more predictable: they will often appeal when they know that the batsman isn't out at all. There is a feeling that if you shout loud enough, often enough, the umpire will have to submit, sooner or later. In the meantime, fury builds up in the bars, where disgruntled supporters may decide to give the umpire a hard time, mockingly calling: 'You're blind!', 'Put your specs on!' or 'Where's your guide dog?'. Umpires do not acknowledge such levity – they are weighed down with dignity (or self-importance), sweaters, caps, spare balls and little stones with which they count the deliveries in each over.

SCORING

In the old days, all you needed to keep the score at a cricket match was a stick and a sharp knife. Each time a run was scored, you cut a notch on your stick. Now you need a computer. This is because of cricket's obsession with statistics. Each time a run is scored the following information must be recorded and be instantly available:

- Team score
- Individual batsman's score
- Number of runs hit off bowler
- Run rate per over
- Strike rate of bowler (the average number of balls bowled per wicket taken)
- Strike rate of batsman (the average number of runs scored per 100 balls faced)
- Run rate required per over by batting side
- Batsman's and bowler's overall averages for this year
- Batsman's and bowler's averages since they were born

- Number of times batsman has hit ball in that direction
- How long since batsman last did that
- How long since bowler last did that. Etc., etc.

It's a bit like the TV broadcasts on election night: too many statistics chasing too little action equals a strong inducement to sleep.

But, should you go to a cricket match, you will see people of all ages assiduously keeping score. Every time the bowler bowls, a dot (no run), a '1' (one run), '2', '3', '4', '6', 'x' (wide), '0' (no-ball), 'w' (wicket) is recorded – against batsman's and bowler's names. And the total score is continuously marked. If a wicket falls, the following details are recorded:

- How the batsman was out
- Who the bowler was
- How many runs the batsman got
- Team score when the wicket fell
- Time when the wicket fell.

Always make the point that such persistent monitoring by spectators does not exist in any other sport. You do not see people at Wimbledon, Wentworth or Wembley carrying out similar functions for tennis, golf and football. It is as if nobody trusts anybody at cricket. There are several theories as to why people should go to such trouble. One theory is that it gives spectators something to do and prevents atrophy of the brain cells during bouts of play. Another theory is that international cricket is shot through with betting and bribery – except, of course, when it comes to the English team.

At important cricket matches, the scorers – one for each team – sit in a little box of their own, acknowledging the umpires' signals and keeping very neat records. In club matches, everybody has to take a turn with the scorebook, which becomes increasingly untidy and incomprehensible. Bluffers can take advantage of the disorderly and ill-disciplined nature of this lax record-keeping to significantly enhance their own performances.

SOUNDING AND LOOKING THE PART

LISTEN UP

Test Match Special (*TMS*) on BBC Radio 4 is a godsend to all cricket bluffers. Not only does it help you understand some of those troublesome laws, it can also get you into the swing of talking about cricket. If you haven't played, watched or listened for several years, try to keep *TMS* on during an entire Test match. Five days might seem a long time, but a period of immersion will be of great benefit to the fledgling bluffer. You can always pretend to be doing something else at the time. If you're listening online at the office, don't forget to shuffle some papers occasionally. Intermittent bursts of keyboard activity are also recommended. And try not to shout, wave your arms or clench your fists during moments of excitement. (Don't worry, they don't happen too often.)

In the asides between commentary, you'll gather that each of the experts has his own cricketing history. Fast bowler Jonathan 'Aggers' Agnew played for Leicestershire and, all too briefly, for England. Slow bowler Vic Marks played for Somerset and, a little less briefly, for England.

Batsman Geoff Boycott played for Yorkshire and England, forever…and ever.

While it's important for bluffers to build up their own back stories, only an extreme bluffer would pretend that they'd played professionally. None of the aforementioned or, indeed, the two most recent recruits – former England skipper Michael Vaughan and spinner/*Strictly Come Dancing*/*A Question of Sport* star Phil Tufnell (Tuffers) – should be used as examples of cricketers you've played with or against. They are far too high-profile.

However, Henry Blofeld, who calls everyone 'dear old thing' in very fruity tones and talks a lot about buses and pigeons, has been in the game so long that you could probably get away with claiming to have been on the same pitch at some time in the past. Popularly known as 'Blowers', he is an Old Etonian and was allegedly the most promising schoolboy cricketer of his generation. But he was run over by a bus and never recaptured his early brilliance. This isn't widely known and is therefore a useful nugget of information to drop into any conversation involving *TMS*. It might also explain his obsession with commenting on buses passing the cricket ground. Another Blofeld bit of trivia is that his father and Ian Fleming were contemporaries at Eton, hence the provenance of the name of the evil mastermind in the Bond books.*

Following the final innings of his fellow veteran of the commentary team, the late Christopher Martin-Jenkins

* For more 007-related bluffing, see *The Bluffer's Guide to Bond*.

(CMJ), Blowers is one of the few surviving career journalists on *TMS*. Former professional cricketers eventually realised that broadcasting is itself a bluff from which they could easily profit, and now the likes of Aggers, Beefy, Bumble and Tuffers call the shots.

'I WAS THERE'

Cricket fans like talking about matches they've seen, players they've met, games they've played and games they're about to play. So an all-round bluffer needs a memorable anecdote. Depending on your age, this can go back up to 50 years.

Suppose that you were born in 1967. You will of course recall that your father took you to see part of the 1976 West Indies tour of England. It was thrilling to witness skipper Clive Lloyd, 'Master Blaster' Viv Richards and that terrifying posse of fast bowlers demolish England at the start of what was to be more than a decade of world domination. Although you were only nine, you remember the final Test at the Oval as if it were yesterday. How could you forget Michael Holding ('Whispering Death') spreadeagling the stumps of England captain Tony 'Hubris' Greig? (Any memory lapse can be rectified on YouTube). Greig had said he was going to make the West Indies grovel. He didn't.

You might also remember being told some of your father's greatest cricketing memories. Let's say he was a Sussex supporter who idolised Ted Dexter, one of the most imperious batsmen of his generation. He was thrilled to have seen 'Lord' Ted's greatest innings at Lord's in 1963 when he treated the murderous West Indian fast-bowling duo of Wes Hall and Charlie Griffith with disdain. 'The Old Man said that the faster they bowled the more savagely he cut, drove and pulled them. Shame Ted wasn't around in '76.'

You will also want to underline your more recent credentials, perhaps with a bit of 2009 Ashes action involving another aspect of play. 'The best bit of fielding I ever saw was when Flintoff ran out Ponting at the Oval in the fifth Test. Freddie may have been past his best as a batsman and bowler but, good grief, that throw from mid-on was awesome. It hit the stumps like an Exocet, leaving Ponting a yard short. You really had to be there.'

Note that the phrase 'You really had to be there' is a useful part of any cricketing bluffer's lexicon. You can even convince yourself that you were. (Freddie's throw is also on YouTube.)

'I PLAYED A BIT, TOO'

Inventing a playing past carries more risk – especially if you are too specific. An over-ambitious bluff might result in an unwelcome response, for example: 'I was actually at the match that day but I certainly don't remember your match-saving cameo.'

The best advice is to avoid claims that can easily be disproved, which means steering clear of anything that could have been officially recorded. Any mention of playing for a county at senior level, for instance, would be suicide. Recalling a trial for a county as a teenager is a possibility. As a schoolboy you may even have batted against a professional in the nets.

'I'm not sure how hard D'Oliveira was trying but he seemed a bit put out when I drove him back over his head. Good old "Dolly" did knock out my middle peg next ball, mind you.' There's another useful lesson here: always admit to some vulnerability when making a major claim like this. An admission that you were 'skittled' next ball will lend conviction to your story. And, at all costs, remember who your chosen professional played for, and where you faced him in the nets.

'You really had to be there' is a useful part of any cricketing bluffer's lexicon. You can even convince yourself that you were.

Tales of glory in faraway places may also be worth a try. But proceed cautiously.

Bluffer (B) Have you ever been to Tasmania?

Rapt Listener (RL) No.

B Lovely island. I was lucky enough to play a bit of grade cricket there.

RL That's quite high standard, isn't it?

B (modestly) Not bad. Not quite professional but not that far off.

RL Did you meet any top players?

B One or two. Have you met any Aussie pros?

RL No.

B I once played against David Boon in a friendly. Bowled him, actually, although he was only a youngster at the time.

RL Really?

B He was probably expecting something quicker. Not that I was slow in those days. Before my shoulder injury, I was measured at more than 70mph. Can't quite reach that these days, of course.

Note that the bluffer at least checked that the 'bluffee' didn't have first-hand experience of Tasmanian cricket. Detailed questions about Tasmanian leagues, grounds and players might have proved awkward. Reference to an injury is another useful tactic. It can help explain why you never reached the highest level. Another possible explanation is a growth spurt; the career of many a promising bowler has stalled after struggling to deliver the ball effectively from a greater height.

Other bluffers, though, will doubtless claim that they were too busy running the country or making a fortune to spend as much time as they would have liked, or indeed their talent deserved, on a cricket pitch.

IF THE CAP FITS...

If claims of straight driving Dolly over his head or clean bowling David Boon spread, an invitation to play will become almost inevitable. Sunday teams are always on the lookout for such players. The wise bluffer will plead injury and rest on his dodgy laurels. For others, though, it will be an irresistible challenge. Some of us just can't say no. If you want to avoid falling at the first hurdle, you'll need some luck as well as some convincing gear.

The bat

You can spend hundreds of pounds on the sort of bat that many professionals use nowadays which seem to be all 'sweet spot'. Bluffers should bear in mind that sweet spots are only relevant if you connect. Since, in the space of a few myopic wafts at mid-air, you'll probably end up looking rather foolish, you'd be better off plumping for a worn model which hints at past triumphs. Try to remove some of the more obvious marks from the edges so that you can maintain the impression that you normally hit the ball off the middle of the bat – even when walking back to the pavilion having been bowled first ball.

The sweater

Without being clearly identifiable as representative of a particular club/county/country, this classic bit of cricketing kit should suggest pedigree. Look around charity shops and car boot sales and you might find a threadbare, disintegrating, stripy number which belonged to a former first 11 player of a now defunct minor public school. If a suitable opportunity arises, state that you were wearing it when you scored your first 'ton' (100 runs), and that it has become your talisman ever since. Cricketers are a superstitious lot and your claim will be met with understanding nods of approval.

The cap

Forget anything with wildlife on it – especially lions (England), bears (Warwickshire), dragons (Somerset), foxes (Leicestershire) or martlets (Sussex). At all costs avoid springboks (South African) and kangaroos and emus (Australian). Roses (red or white) should also be avoided. Nobody will believe that you have earned any of the above, so go for a sponsor's logo; beer companies are quite useful. Anything faded and well-worn will help you look the part.

The trousers

Not too smart but suggesting past action in the line of duty. A few assiduously applied grass stains should do the trick. Opt for cream flannels if you want to attract the admiring attentions of Lily Rose Cooper.

The blazer

A blazer is a necessary part of the bluffer's wardrobe. You can afford to make a statement here, and you'll know if it has the right impact when people gasp involuntarily and shield their eyes. Find the most hideously colour-clashing sartorial fashion crime you can lay your hands on, and if it isn't already well-worn (suggesting a strong cricketing pedigree), send it to yourself via the Royal Mail a couple of times. This will ensure that it receives the required degree of the fashionable 'distressed' look. If asked about the garment's provenance, say confidently that it is the team blazer of the 'Devils', an allegedly well-known team of cricketing mavericks in Tasmania.

Never be afraid to drop the name of this Australian island state into any cricket bluffing conversation – it's so far away that few people are likely to know much about it. This is why there are frequent references to it in this guide.

The protection

The choice of protective gear depends on which parts of the body you hold most dear, but it's worth buying some decent pads, some batting gloves and, if you're male, a 'box' (the reinforced codpiece which protects the most vital part of your anatomy). Most Sunday sides have a sweaty team bag with pads and other odds and ends in various states of decay among the mice droppings, so it is always a good idea to wear your own box. You might also want to make sure the spare team helmet fits while you watch the opposition's fast bowler steam in.

If you can get away with it, the best advice is to place yourself where the ball seldom comes. The less you see of the action, the greater your chances of sustaining the bluff.

ON THE PITCH

You've exaggerated your cricketing past, you've bought some kit and you're now deeply regretting accepting that invitation to play. You've rushed in where angels fear to tread. You might be forgiven for swerving into the nearest pub on your way to the village ground. A phone call to cry off followed by a few restorative pints is probably the sensible option. But the beer might actually embolden you. After all, it's only a village game, you will tell yourself, and didn't you once deceive David Boon with your slower ball and tonk D'Oliveira back over his head? Well, actually no, but the ale has worked its magic and you've managed to convince yourself that you did.

BATTING

Your faded cap, free of beastly insignia, may hint of many distinguished innings in the past, but having seen the opposition fast bowler, you're now seriously considering the sweaty club helmet.

There have already been raised eyebrows that the

former child prodigy who once got the better of famous professional cricketers has resisted offers to open the batting. Instead, realising the folly of your bluff, you've been arguing strenuously to go in at number 11 (also known as 'last' – a position in the batting order that suggests that little is expected of you). Your skipper is having none of it: 'You may be a little rusty but let's have no false modesty. I've put you down at six and please go easy on the bowling. I don't want to be accused of playing a ringer.'

Loosen your shoulders by swinging the bat a couple of times. All professionals do this, so you should too.

The only remaining option, apart from slamming your fingers in the car door, is to face the consequences of your bluff. The good news is that most Sunday village sides seldom have more than one quick bowler. Indeed, most are, in varying degrees, really rather slow. (But beware of the invitingly slow ball; the temptation to come charging out of your crease to belt it into the pub car park has been the undoing of many.)

Walking out to the crease, you should at least look the part. Loosen your shoulders by swinging the bat a couple of times. All professionals do this, so you should too. Stride towards your fate like a cricketing god. Once at the wicket, survey the field by nodding at various positions as if committing them to memory. Then try to boost yourself psychologically by drawing on past successes. As these probably won't involve cricket, look back on any other positive achievements in your life. If you don't have any, convince yourself that this is your opportunity to redress the balance.

Now you're in the right frame of mind, hold your bat in front of middle stump and say: 'Middle, please, umpire.' This is called 'taking your guard' and, depending on your umpire's eyesight, ensures that your bat is firmly grounded directly in front of the stumps. One final look around and then you concentrate on the ball. Once it's on the way, step aside with a flourish. If it hits the stumps, say 'well bowled' and walk off smartly.

Misjudgments, even by those who've faced a Test bowler, are not uncommon at the start of an innings and can be forgiven. But it's much more likely that the ball will miss the stumps by some distance. Your flourish may then look like a judicious 'leave', in which case you can try to hit the next one. If that hits the bat and finds a gap through the fielders, blaze away. It could just be your day.

BOWLING

Your teammates know that you were once a legend in Tasmania but, as you've had to explain several times, that was before the injury that ended your fast-bowling career. Despite this setback and the decades that have passed since, the captain insists that you have an over or two. You have one advantage. Word of your exploits has reached the opposing side and their batsmen are understandably nervous. Attack while you can. Position several fielders close to the bat and mark out a very long run-up. The batsman facing will be in a state of jellified paralysis (if there is such a condition). Having given him your meanest look, race up to the wicket and release.

Expecting a ball of lethal speed, he will be quite unprepared for the harmless lob that follows. With luck, it might be straight and gently nudge the stumps, dislodging the bails – in which case you will be engulfed by members of your team demanding a 'high five' (this is how modern cricketers applaud a wicket). If, on the other hand, the ball trickles uselessly past the stumps, rub your back, apologise to the bewildered batsman and continue the over, explaining that you felt a 'twinge' and that you're now going to have to bowl slowly. Switch the field to extreme defensive mode by dispatching everyone to the boundary. Take heart; in Sunday cricket, it's almost always the bad balls that take wickets. If your luck continues, your fielders will catch some of the mistimed slogs and you could end up with a hatful.

FIELDING

Bluffing at fielding is easier than bluffing at batting or bowling. Even the most lithe of professional fielders often struggle in later years.

Even so, it might be better not to attempt to throw 'overarm' as your clueless style will probably give you away.

Catching is more problematic. A good catcher usually stays a good catcher. If the ball whizzes past you like a bullet, the best policy is to pretend not to have seen it. You can blame the sun (if there is any), a difficult background (cloud, trees), passing flying insects or failing eyesight. If the ball is 'skyed' and you look like being the nearest fielder to it, run like hell in the opposite direction and shout: 'Yours!'. By the time it lands you will have distanced yourself sufficiently from the drop zone.

If you can get away with it, the best advice is to place yourself where the ball seldom comes. The less you see of the action, the greater your chances of sustaining the bluff.

UMPIRING

The laws of cricket are rather like Serbo-Croat grammar – almost impossible to grasp. Just when you think you've got it, an exception rears its head. In particular, lbw is as slippery as a Slavic subjunctive or that bit about indirect objects and past participles. For example: a batsman can't be out lbw if the ball pitches outside the stumps, unless he's not playing a stroke, and then he can only be out if it pitches outside the off stump, and then only if the ball is going on to hit the wicket. You'd be better off learning irregular verbs in Serbo-Croat.

Luckily, there's no need to worry. Many professionals don't have much of a clue either. When umpiring a village game, simply turn down all lbw appeals unless the batsman is on the back foot and plumb in front of middle stump. If asked why, just say 'missing leg' or 'too high'.

Whenever you're asked to adjudicate – be it an lbw, a catch or a possible run out – the crucial thing is to appear decisive even though you're probably wrong.

PUBBING

This is one area where amateurs can compete with professionals. Any harsh words that may have been said during the heat of battle are usually forgotten. Jugs of beer are manfully consumed and post-match analysis will blur into a kind of bluffers' conspiracy. The batsman bowled by a rotten delivery will agree with the bowler that it was an unplayable ball. Tipsily, history is rewritten:

Batsman Not even Boycott could have kept that out.

Bowler It was my outswinger with some nip back off the pitch.

Batsman There's no shame in being bowled by a jaffa like that.

Bowler None at all. And you were going well until then.

Batsman I was especially pleased with that lofted drive. Did you see that the fielder never even got a hand to it?

Bowler Super shot, that. I gather that you once played grade cricket in Tasmania.

The great thing about post-match pub bluffing is that you are absolutely safe in the company of fellow bluffers. Everyone just wants to carry on bluffing. 'Same again please, Landlord!'

EXCUSES

Defeated batsmen

'It moved an absolute mile.' (bowled)

'It was a vicious daisy-cutter. Never bounced.' (bowled)

'It hit a stone and reared up at my throat.' (caught)

'A wasp flew into my visor.' (hit wicket)

'I thought the umpire said "no-ball."' (bowled after an injudicious swipe)

'It swung so much I did well to get a touch on it.' (caught in the slips)

'I heard the bowler was having a family crisis so I surrendered my wicket to cheer him up.' (bowled, lbw, hit wicket, played on, caught, run out or stumped)

Fumbling fielders

'I lost it in the trees/bushes/crowd/freak typhoon.'

'The sun was glinting off a car windscreen.'

'These new contact lenses are hopeless.'

Terrible bowling

'I think I've done my hamstring.'

'The ball's been tampered with.'

'I could feel it coming right just as the skipper took me off.'

'I should have had four wickets. There was a missed stumping and three dropped catches.'

Batting can induce a delusional state which, in the heat of the moment, causes certain players to deny irrefutable evidence of their downfall.

PROFESSIONAL BLUFFING

While village cricket bumbles on in much the same way as it's always done, recent changes in the international game have made life much harder for the Test match bluffer. Under DRS (the Decision Review System), lbws and catches can now be checked by the third umpire (if he's awake) with the aid of a ball-tracking gizmo called 'Hawkeye' and infrared imaging called 'Hotspot'. As well as correcting some glaring umpiring errors, this has exposed a great deal of bluffing among batters, bowlers and fielders. Some might even view the introduction of modern technology to be in direct contravention of the spirit of the game. After all, few games lend themselves as willingly to bluffing as cricket, so why ruin a good thing?

BLUFFING BATSMEN

The first cricketing superstar, WG Grace, was, it seems, not so much a bluffer as an outright cheat. He once refused to leave the crease, after being given out lbw, with the words: 'They came to watch me bat, not you bowl.' On another occasion when a bowler removed his bails, he replaced them, saying: 'The wind's strong today, umpire.'

Modern batsmen, to give them credit, are a little more subtle. When the bowler hits them on the glove and the ball is caught by the wicketkeeper ('out' caught behind), they might rub an elbow vigorously to indicate another point of contact. When they're hit on the pad in front of the stumps ('plumb' lbw), they might rub a thigh to fool the umpire into thinking that the ball struck them higher than it did. A faint nick to the slips or wicketkeeper may find them pointing to a pad or some other item of apparel to suggest an alternative source of the guilty-sounding noise.

After edging to the slips or wicketkeeper, a seasoned bluffer will resist the instinct to look behind. An involuntary backward glance is usually a sure sign of guilt.

Batting can induce a delusional state which, in the heat of the moment, causes certain players to deny irrefutable evidence of their downfall. They seem capable of bluffing even themselves. An egotistical batsman might harbour the thought that a lesser talent doesn't deserve to get them out. Such self-belief may help a player on the road to stardom but block his path to greatness. The South African-born England batsman (there are many), Kevin Pietersen, has been defeated a disproportionate number of times by left-arm spin. Denying any weakness, he has probably convinced himself there isn't a problem.

With the advent of DRS, umpires seem more willing to pass the death sentence. In the past, batsmen were always given the benefit of the doubt. Now, they don't escape the noose so easily. If they choose to review a decision which, on replay, is marginal, the benefit is given to the umpire.

Resist the instinct to look behind. An involuntary backward glance is usually a sure sign of guilt.

The point of the system is to correct an obvious mistake, in which case the decision can be reversed. As players become more familiar with DRS, it could encourage more sophisticated forms of bluffing. For example, both batting and fielding sides are usually allowed two 'reviews' of a decision in each innings. When an umpire rejects an appeal from the fielding side, the batsman could give the impression that he might actually have been 'out' and thus trick the opposition into wasting a review. This is where cricket bluffing becomes fiendishly complicated.

BLUFFING BOWLERS

Bowlers – spin bowlers in particular – are often great bluffers. None more so than the Australian master of the art, Shane Warne, who, tellingly, has spent a lot of time at the poker table since he gave up Test cricket. 'Warnie' was always pretending that he'd mastered a new mystery ball which would destroy the opposition, even though he did that effectively enough with his conventional leg spin anyway. His talk of sliders, zooters and zingers bamboozled both batsmen and commentators and left us armchair bluffers mightily confused. England batting coach Graham Gooch, who played Warne better than most, loftily dismissed his 'inventions' as 'smoke and mirrors'. Former England and Middlesex captain Mike Gatting, who was bowled by Warne's 'ball of the century', might disagree.

The best spinners vary the flight of the ball and the degree and direction of turn when it bounces. Sometimes a batsman can read what's going to happen from the bowler's action. Mostly, especially if he's English, he doesn't have a clue. Great spinners can move the ball both ways with a similar action. The Pakistani off-spinner Saqlain Mushtaq developed a ball called the '*doosra*' (Urdu for 'the second one') which looked the same as his stock delivery but wasn't. He also spoke of a '*teesra*' ('the third one'). One of his successors, Saeed Ajmal, once destroyed the England team with, seemingly, impenetrably disguised fourth and fifth ones.

The godfather of bluffing spinners was Bernard Bosanquet, father of the late, lamented newsreader Reggie. Bernard invented the ball known as the 'googly' (originally called the 'Bosie'). The googly is an off break bowled with a leg-break action. In other words, instead of spinning away from a right-handed batsman, as he might expect from the action, it spins towards him. An ace bluffer, Bosanquet would behave as though this was an accidental, freak delivery. It was only with the passage of time that cricketers realised he could bowl it intentionally. Bosie, unlike Warnie, was an erratic bowler (it clearly ran in the family, Reggie often reading the news while somewhat over-refreshed). Nevertheless, Bosie played regularly for Middlesex and seven times for England and was, by all accounts, a more than useful batsman.

BLUFFING FIELDERS

In general, the captain or bowler places the fielders where he thinks the ball is most likely to go. But cricket, being a game of bluff, is not quite as simple as that. A fielder may be switched to a position to make the batsman think the bowler is going to bowl in a certain way when the bowler has precisely the opposite intention. Thus a fielder may be directed to a spot on the boundary where a batsman might expect to hit a high-bouncing short ball. The batsman, seeing the change in field, will expect such a ball but might, instead, receive a full, low non-bouncing ball (or 'yorker' – *see* 'Glossary', page 114) which could spell his dismissal.

In the same way, a batsman might pretend to advance down the pitch and then step back, hoping that the bowler will be fooled into bowling a short ball which will be easy to hit.

Often the wicketkeeper is the noisiest and, from the batsman's point of view, most irritating fielder. When he's not appealing for catches and stumpings, he'll be saying something to try to put the batsman off. He may try to exaggerate the talents of the bowler or the dangers of the pitch. If he's Australian, expect straightforward abuse – often, but not always, questioning the batsman's sexuality or his wife's fidelity (*see* 'Sledging' in 'The Global Game: Australia', page 76).

For all the benefits of technology, there can still be uncertainty about whether a fielder has fairly caught a ball. Cameras don't seem able to determine reliably whether a ball has been caught on the full (out) or has touched the ground before being caught (not out). The fielder may claim the catch, leaving the third umpire to decide whether it's a bluff. Since the cameras often make it seem as if the ball has bounced, the batsman usually gets the benefit of the doubt in this instance (probably unfairly).

BLUFFING COMMENTATORS

Commentators, tending to be former professional cricketers, aren't above a bit of bluffing themselves. Any immediate recall of multiple facts should alert suspicion. Of course they are, in the main, vastly knowledgeable, having forfeited family life to travel the world in pursuit of men playing around with a little red ball. But sometimes you can't help suspect that they're cheating like naughty schoolboys – being fed information which they give the impression of having already known. Even on *TMS*, obscure facts sometimes seem to flow a little too freely from those formidable cricketing brains. Let's tune in:

> 'Oh dear, he's out without scoring for the second time in the match. What an unfortunate Test debut. Of course,

Tremlett also bagged a pair on debut against India at Lord's in 2007.'

Impressive recall, but then there's more:

'Before that it was Gavin Hamilton against South Africa in 1999 and then, of course, Graham Gooch in '75 at Edgbaston against Australia.'

Your admiration increases.

'And then there was poor old Jim Smith in 1934 at Bridgetown against the West Indies.'

Doubt sets in.

'And before that Fred Grace, brother of WG, against Australia at the Oval in 1880.'

Now, not even the most formidable cricket buffs would get all five. He's definitely got a crib sheet.

Some radio commentators also seem to have the ability to describe a confusing flash of action with almost instant clarity. Perhaps this is thanks to a mystical sixth sense honed over years of playing and watching. More likely, they've just seen a TV replay.

Former cricketers turned commentators can usually be relied on to remember their own past triumphs; however, they may be more reticent about their failures. For example, the fact that Sky TV pundits Nasser Hussain and Ian Botham were the last two England captains to get 'ducks' (no runs) in both innings of a Test match is something you may not have heard trumpeted on Sky.

For the record, Hussain 'bagged' his pair – getting two consecutive ducks in the same match – against the West Indies at the Oval in 2000, while Botham did the double at Lord's against Australia in 1981. In fairness, though, Beefy did rather make amends with some match-winning exploits later in the series. Viewers may occasionally be reminded of that.

CRICKET IN ALL ITS FORMS

Only the most reckless bluffer will go on the attack straight away. The less you know, the more you're at risk of exposure, so those of a more sensible disposition are unlikely to open their innings by claiming to have bowled an Australian Test player with a well-disguised slower ball in Tasmania, or hoicked an English Test player out of the ground at Worcester. That's for later. Wiser backseat bluffers will want to play themselves in first.

As you'll have already gathered, this will involve listening to *TMS* and watching some televised cricket as well. Unless you're a naturally gifted sportsman, it definitely won't involve courting certain humiliation and probable injury by prematurely and foolishly accepting an invitation to play.

A more helpful early step would be to watch some live cricket at county or international level. Bluffers will feel on safer ground having seen part of a four-day county game, Twenty20 bash or, if finances allow, some Test cricket (maximum duration five days).

In the stands, it's all about giving the impression of being a knowledgeable observer. Sometimes a well-timed shrug, sigh or snort may be enough. Then, when you've got your eye in, you can attempt some more adventurous bluffs. The key for novices is to minimise the chances of saying or doing the wrong thing. An inexperienced spectator should play with a reasonably straight bat (*see* 'Glossary', page 113).

Different bluffs apply to different forms of the game. Try not to mix them up, because that will give the game away faster than a late-order England batting collapse.

FOUR-DAY COUNTY GAME

This is where you will find the hardy, all-weather fans who have followed their chosen county for most of their lives, probably wearing the same anorak. They will have enjoyed the ups but also the downs, taking grim satisfaction in detailing the shortcomings of the team in general and individuals in particular. 'He's never an opener,' you might hear someone say. 'Look at him wafting away outside off stump, feet nowhere near the ball. He'll be lucky to still be there at the end of the over if the bowling's up to anything.'

It's the kind of classic win-win remark that could prove useful to any bluffer. For if the opener does get out quickly, the gloom-monger will be proved right and, if he doesn't, it'll be the bowlers' fault.

Meanwhile, as the April wind howls through the stands and the fielders rub their frozen hands, you might wonder if you wouldn't have been better off learning to bluff about a less exposed sport – indoor bowls, perhaps. You may also be puzzled about the apparent lack of activity. But, unless you're intending to be provocative, avoid repeating Groucho Marx's quip an hour or so into his first (and last) cricket match: 'This is great. When does it start?'

You might be surprised (and relieved) to discover that a lot of talk at a cricket match doesn't actually involve cricket. In fact, it's far more likely to be about the weather. So a passing knowledge of meteorology will stand you in good stead. Speculation about the next rain shower, where it's coming from, and with what force, is a perennial cricketing standby.

You might be surprised (and relieved) to discover that a lot of talk at a cricket match doesn't actually involve cricket.

Since county cricket watchers are often impressed by any signs of insider knowledge, you might even go off on a slight tangent, mentioning, for example, that weather presenter John Kettley was a fairly decent league cricketer:

'He used to play for Todmorden which, as you know, is the only Yorkshire side in the Lancashire League.'

'Really?'

'Yes, John was quite a useful bowler.' (Note the use of the first name, suggesting familiarity).

'Did you ever play against him?'

'Just the once, but I think he must have been having an off-day.'

'Really?'

'I managed to hit him out of the attack. It's the only time I've scored more than 20 in an over.'

'I bet he's never forgiven you.'

'He's probably forgotten all about me. Todmorden were a good side in those days, mind you. Brian Close was their pro.'

At which point the sensible bluffer will quit while he's ahead. In fact, he probably should have stopped after that gem about the Lancashire League.

The temptation to cross the line from sensible to reckless can be strong but it's nowhere near as dangerous as 'walking behind the bowler's arm'. This is just about the most heinous crime a spectator can commit in any form of cricket and will unleash a stream of bile from even the most mild-mannered anorak. They may not have been watching but will be infuriated by any interruption in play. The bowler, especially if he's got a run-up of 50 yards or more, will threaten to throttle you or worse. He'll have to start his run-up again, the batsman having stepped aside after being distracted by your movement. The umpire will probably give you a ticking off, too. In fact, you may as well go home.

TWENTY20

This is like four-day cricket in fast forward. It is the shortest version of competitive cricket, lasting about four hours on average. This is lightning fast in cricket terms, but still more than twice the length of a normal football or rugby match.

For a batsman, moving your feet isn't as important as giving the ball a good whack. For a spectator, there's little time to dwell on the finer points of the game; they are better advised to keep an eye on the action to avoid being hit by a ball heading in their direction.

The MCC coaching manual has certainly taken a battering, with Twenty20 showing contempt for the orthodox technique. Batsmen will scoop the ball over their heads or switch from hitting it right-handed to left-handed. For a new breed of cricketers, this is the future of cricket. So where should the bluffer stand?

Well, frankly, anything goes. Depending on your neighbour and the state of the match, you can argue that the Vandals are at the gates or that the shorter form has revived the game's flagging fortunes (a better line during an exciting game). What is beyond doubt is that you can take a wild verbal swipe and miss, and no one will hold it against you. Rather like Twenty20 itself.

TEST CRICKET

Many bluffers will have vague childhood memories of being dragged along to a Test match with their father or other male *in loco parentis* – sitting, perhaps, on a hard seat on a cold day and watching nothing much happening. Given that he occupied the crease for decades, chances are you will have seen the gripping spectacle of Geoffrey Boycott blocking interminably. But it's unlikely you'll remember anything in particular, except a lingering feeling of boredom and resentment.

Test match cricket is different now. Bluffers should never buy a ticket for the fifth day as games seldom last that long. The Decision Review System, coupled with a growing recklessness among batsmen (a result possibly of Twenty20), means that Test matches are seldom drab affairs. They are not cheap either. Having paid the better part of £100 for your travel and ticket to Lord's, you may want to avoid saying: 'The next round's on me.'

Before indulging in any serious Test match bluffing, you'll need to size up your fellow spectators. Beware, for example, of the tie-wearing blazer brigade, especially if they're also equipped with a scorebook and a pair of binoculars. They're almost certainly better bluffers than you.

It's a sign of the growing popularity of cricket that some people will go to a Lord's Test match simply because they think it's the place to be. This lot deserves your full repertoire plus any inspired, alcohol-fuelled embellishments. While you should stop short of claiming that you've actually played Test cricket, schoolboy triumphs and a regular 'knock' for the Tassie Devils are unlikely to be challenged.

Meanwhile, you might have noticed the clusters of people with their backs to the cricket in ruinously expensive hospitality boxes. If you ever manage to bluff your way in, brush up on tax avoidance schemes and investment opportunities. Cricket is unlikely ever to be discussed.

Noisy fans in the cheaper seats may belong to the 'Barmy Army' which has become almost as much a cricketing institution as the MCC. At every Test ground except Lord's, the army will have its own section in the stands. Look out for the Cross of St George flags, banners, football shirts, chain mail and large plastic swords. Listen out for the chants and songs (hard to avoid without state-of-the-art noise-cancelling earphones). A well-organised group with its own website, they follow the English team around the world, often outnumbering the opposition's supporters. Their trumpeter, Billy Cooper, has played in front of larger crowds than most of the world's leading musicians. Attempting to bluff a member of the 'Army' would be an act of absurd bravery and possibly a stupid one too.

THE AMATEUR GAME

You will be required to know all about the different levels of cricket. We can only include the essentials of the amateur game as it is played in Britain. On a wider geographical scale it is safe to make up what you want about different countries' cricketing structures. Unless, of course, you happen to be talking to a citizen of the country in question (or one nearby).

LEAGUE CRICKET

This is played throughout Britain, but the most famous is the Lancashire League. Small towns in Lancashire each employ one professional cricketer, often a player of international stature who may be seeking domestic qualification to play for an English county. It may sound a bit like Gulliver among the Lilliputians, but Lancashire is a very tough cricketing county and has produced such heroes as AC MacLaren, whose 424 is still the highest individual first-class score on an English ground; George Duckworth, whose appeal is the loudest recorded on any English ground; and Eddie Paynter, whose temperature of 102°F is the highest registered at a Test match wicket.

CLUB CRICKET

This, too, is played all over Britain. It is the backbone of the game and, possibly, of the entire sociopolitical structure of the country. Thus it has much to answer for. Club cricket comes in three varieties:

Suburban Very smart. Everyone wears white. Times, laws and customs are all scrupulously observed. Grounds are neatly kept, well-equipped and jealously guarded from all forms of building development. The cricket is as neat as cucumber sandwiches. There is an annual dinner (stag and a bit naughty) and an annual dance (mixed and not at all naughty).

Village/rural Not so smart, though a real attempt is made to provide adequate kit and equipment. The setting is idyllic but since the ground has to serve so many other purposes (football, dog exercising, boot sales, village fête, etc.) the pitch will be 'sporting' and the outfield a mass of holes, bumps, nettles, cowpats and strange rural artefacts. The cricket is as lusty as the players.

Municipal A very casual affair. Scratch teams play occasional games on grounds owned by the local council. Pitch and outfield are lethally rough. Nobody wears white, 'tea' consists of crates of lager and bags of doughnuts, and there is an outstanding lack of skill.

SCHOOLS CRICKET

State education has more or less given up cricket. It is expensive, needs a great deal of space and hours and hours of time, does not do a lot for hyperactive inner-city youth, and is not likely to feature in any core curriculum imposed by the secretary of state for education.

So, schools cricket is left to the private sector. At prep school, whole afternoons are given up to coaching: 'Bat and pad together, Tompkins Minor. I'm sure your father isn't paying £3,000 a term to have you flashing at good length balls outside your off stump...What do you mean "it hurt"? It's a cricket ball, for goodness sake! It's supposed to hurt...'

BEACH CRICKET

The rules of beach cricket are simple:

1. If the ball hits the breakwater post anywhere below the line scratched by Uncle Will, you're out.
2. You can't run more than four if the ball goes on the pebbles.

3. You can't expect Auntie Fay to bowl into the wind.
4. If you hit the ball into the sea, you go and get it.
5. Youngest bats first.
6. Strangers aren't invited to play without consulting Mum and Dad.
7. You can't run if Shep goes off with the ball.
8. Only 10 more overs to be bowled after it's dark.

FRENCH CRICKET

This has nothing to do with the French, of course. The phrase comes from the Middle English *frénésie-criquet* ('frenzied cricket') – a suitable name for the non-stop, all-action game where the main object is to break the batsman's leg. The rules of French cricket are more complicated than those of beach cricket, and vary enormously from area to area. These are some currently applicable in the streets behind the Oval:

1. Can't turn round if you didn't hit the ball.
2. One bounce caught one hand is 'out'.
3. Bowl from where the ball stops – no running forward with it.
4. Little Terry mustn't field too near.
5. Over the fence is 'out' and you have to go and ask for the ball back.

6. Mustn't bowl too fast at Mrs Ruxley since her operation.
7. Oldest bats first.
8. On the knee isn't out, unless the batsperson was deliberately crouching.
9. If anything happens to those delphiniums, that's the end of the game.

Australian cricketers invented sledging. It may not be subtle but, judging by their impressive playing record, it seems to work.

THE GLOBAL GAME

Since it is played by both sexes in some of the furthest-flung parts of the world, cricket can be said to be both unisex and multinational. More than 100 countries belong to an ever-expanding cricketing empire which is ruled by blazer-wearing despots from the headquarters of the International Cricket Council (ICC) in Dubai. Why it's in Dubai – not known for its lush, green cricket grounds – nobody is quite sure. As well as the 10 Test-playing nations (full members of the ICC), there were, at the last count, 36 associate members and 60 affiliate members.

The Chinese Cricket Association is nurturing players who, it claims, will help China qualify for the World Cup in 2019. Many of them come from the north-east province of Heilongjiang which borders Russia and Mongolia and is under snow for nearly five months of the year. In 2020, they say, they'll achieve Test status. This could be a bluff, but on the other hand it could be part of a wider strategy for world domination. You should also take note of other more unlikely cricketing outposts including Afghanistan, Bulgaria, Finland, Rwanda and the Turks and Caicos Islands.

The scope for exotic cricketing bluffing is practically limitless. 'We hacked out a pitch in the jungle but just as I was about to complete my 50, a rather peevish gorilla came charging out of the trees...etc., etc.'

A match has also been played at the South Pole (as yet, no ICC status) where, apparently, a team made up of English players beat an outfit from the rest of the world. Think carefully before you claim to have been there. But if you do, say that the minus 40°C temperature froze the film on your eyeballs and contributed to your early dismissal. Don't blame it on the arrival of a marauding polar bear. There aren't any at the South Pole.

MAIN CRICKETING NATIONS

Every cricketing country exhibits a national style. The England team of today may look very different from that of 1859, but it is still essentially English in the way that it plays and behaves. Since we are covering a timespan of 150 years, bluffers can feel free to make sweepingly grand statements. History will provide evidence to back them all.

ENGLAND

Cricketing characteristics:

Batting Majestic. Brittle. Crisis-prone.

Bowling As for batting but omit 'Majestic'.

Fielding Field like tigers, but usually in the wrong position.

Debating point The England side which reached the top of the world's Test rankings in 2011 turned out, in no small measure, to be South African. Pretending to be an Englishman if you're actually a South African is bluffing of the highest order. Both Kevin Pietersen and Jonathan Trott, two of the better batsmen, learnt to play under the African sun.

Pietersen was born in Pietermaritzburg and played for Natal, while Trott was born in Cape Town and played for South Africa at both Under-15 and Under-19 levels. Former captain Andrew Strauss and wicketkeeper Matthew Prior were also born in South Africa, although neither stayed much beyond early childhood.

In the 2011 World Cup, when England needed South Africa to beat Bangladesh to reach the quarter finals, South African captain Graeme Smith remarked: 'English fans are used to supporting South Africans these days.' Resist the temptation to retort: 'Sarky Springbok git.' Bluffers should not stoop to name-calling, however much it is justified.

Note that there is little love lost among South African-born cricketers playing for England. Correction: there is little love lost between Kevin Pietersen ('KP' to his friends and enemies) and the rest of the South African-born cricketers playing for England. During the last Test series between England and South Africa in 2012, when the latter usurped England as the world's number one team, KP was accused of texting his opponents/compatriots about Andrew Strauss's perceived weaknesses as a cricketer and as a captain. The thoroughly decent and noble Strauss retired from cricket shortly afterwards, and KP was promptly dropped from the England Test team – and then hastily reinstated for a tour of India. This little scandal is guaranteed to keep MCC members spluttering and fuming for the next couple of millennia, and so all bluffers are required to know about it.

AUSTRALIA

Cricketing characteristics:

Batting Aim not for victory but for total destruction of the opposition.

Bowling Hunt in pairs – Lindwall and Miller, Lillee and Thomson (amusingly described as 'Lillian Thomson' by England supporters).

Fielding Catch anything. Cavort around the pitch like dervishes.

Debating point The Australians are good at bluffing 'with intent'. Most of their bluffs take the form of threats snarled at opposing batsmen by bowlers or close fielders. In cricket this is called 'sledging' and is done to intimidate and unsettle opponents. Australian cricketers invented it, and all of the best sledging anecdotes involve one of their number. It may not be subtle but, judging by their impressive playing record, it seems to work.

You will be required to know some of the finest examples of the genre. Here's a beaut from Aussie pace bowler Craig McDermott to quaking lower-order batsman Phil Tufnell: 'Hospital food suit you?' The Australian crowds even got on poor Tuffers' back, one spectator shouting: 'Can I borrow your brain, Tufnell? I'm building an idiot.'

Occasionally a batsman will bite back, as in the following exchange between Mark Waugh (slip fielder and twin brother of Aussie captain Steve) and James Ormond, inexperienced England all-rounder:

Waugh F*** me, look who it is. What are you doing out here? There's no way you're good enough to play for England.

Ormond Maybe not. But at least I'm the best player in my family.

One of the wittiest ripostes came from South African batsman Daryll Cullinan in answer to Aussie spinner Shane Warne:

Warne I've waited two years for another chance to humiliate you.

Cullinan Looks like you've spent it eating.

Warne is now a shadow of his former self but, to give that classic quote some context, in 1996 even his own wicketkeeper Ian Healy said: 'Shane Warne's idea of a balanced diet is a cheeseburger in each hand.'

The Australians seem to reserve their most vicious sledging for the English. Perhaps it all goes back to the Bodyline tour. On one heart-stopping occasion English speedster Harold Larwood felled Aussie skipper Bill Woodfull with a brutal short ball. Apparently, England's inscrutable captain Douglas Jardine remarked mildly:

'Well bowled, Harold.'

Jardine later complained to Woodfull that an Australian player had called one of his bowlers a bastard. Woodfull supposedly turned to his team and said words to the effect of: 'Which one of you bastards called this bastard's bowler a bastard?'

The Australians should be congratulated for enriching the game with such colourful language. Not least because it has a tendency to rebound on them. Here's a final example (but there are many more). Australian fast bowler Glenn McGrath to Zimbabwean bowler Eddo Brandes:

McGrath Why are you so fat?

Brandes (reportedly) Because every time I f*** your wife she gives me a biscuit.

INDIA

Cricketing characteristics:

Batting Supple and subtle. Not much sledgehammer. On the other hand they didn't need it with the diminutive Sachin Tendulkar, the highest scorer of all time in Test cricket.

Bowling Supreme in spin. Typical analyses: 103 overs, 92 maidens, 15 runs, 1 wicket; or 12 overs, 0 maidens, 163 runs, 8 wickets. Or in the case of Anil Kumble, one of the greatest tweakers ever, how about an analysis of bowling out the entire Pakistan team single-handedly in 1999?

Fielding Often give the impression that they are not interested in it.

Debating point Separating bluff from reality in India, for outsiders at least, seems impossible. Is the influence of illegal bookmakers really as great as they claim? Why is the team so brilliant at home and hopeless abroad? Do the fans really mean it when they threaten the lives of players who've upset them?

The brave bluffer may claim inside knowledge on these questions but would be wise to check first that he or she is not speaking to an ICC undercover investigator.

The Indian Premier League (IPL), a televised Twenty20 spectacle for some of the world's most talented cricketers, is pure cricket bling. Some top Indian players are treated like gods with the result that many of them believe that they are.

PAKISTAN

Cricketing characteristics:

Batting: Constantly finding gifted prodigies.

Bowling: Keep alive the art of wrist spin bowling, for which they are to be deeply thanked. And every now and then they come up with a truly terrifying left-arm quickie like Wasim Akram, or a truly terrifyingly attractive-to-women (especially to British billionaires' daughters) all-rounder like Imran Khan.

Fielding: Very good, when they take their hands out of their pockets in time.

Debating point: A recent scandal involving three Pakistani Test stars resulted in prison sentences for the guilty parties. A video, posted by a now defunct tabloid newspaper, showed a sports agent predicting that one of the bowlers would bowl a no-ball at specific times during the game, which he duly did. Bowlers often bowl no-balls (one assumes unintentionally), but now every time a no-ball is delivered, an odd rustle can be heard in the crowd. It's usually people checking their betting slips.

SRI LANKA

Cricketing characteristics:

Batting: Either swashbuckling and effective, or swashbuckling and not.

Bowling: Mercurial and unreadable. *See* 'Debating point' below.

Fielding: Not bad, but a definite air of wanting to be doing anything but.

Debating point: An interesting controversy into which bluffers might be tempted to venture is: was the highest ever wicket-taker in Test cricket a 'chucker'? A chucker, you will need to know, is a bowler who throws the ball rather than bowls it with a straight arm. An endless debate surrounds the Sri Lankan superstar Muttiah Muralitharan, or 'Murali' as he's better known. If he did throw rather than bowl the ball and get away with it, it has to be one of the more remarkable bluffs in the history of cricket.

A bowler is not supposed to straighten his arm before release, although to a greater or lesser degree most do. Slow bowler Murali has freakishly flexible wrists and shoulders. This allows him to bowl like a triple-jointed contortionist, making his action look particularly suspect as well as enabling him to spin the ball on all surfaces.

From the start of his stellar career in 1992 to its finish in 2011, there were constant doubts about its legality. A series of biomechanical tests concluded that a congenital defect created the illusion of throwing – a defect most cricketers would die for. The ICC backed Murali and increased the angle that bowlers are allowed to straighten their arms to 15 degrees. Throughout his career, Australians in particular gave Murali stick. Even the then prime minister John Howard called him a chucker.

Others, though, marvelled at his ability. In 2002, *Wisden* ranked him the best bowler of all time. Bluffers should also note that he's the only bowler to have taken 10 or more wickets in a match against all other Test-playing nations (a snippet that should impress someone, but probably not on a first date).

NEW ZEALAND

Cricketing characteristics:

Batting: Tend to rely on one or two charismatic players (in short supply).

Bowling: All Kiwi bowlers are medium-fast. Opponents aren't dismissed, they succumb to boredom.

Fielding: Awesomely keen. Not always awesomely effective.

Debating point: Cricketers in New Zealand can be rather underwhelming, apart from a few individual greats headed by Richard Hadlee, a dashing, mustachioed bowling all-rounder of the 1970s and 1980s who resembled Errol Flynn. Their finest batsman in recent times was Martin Crowe, a cousin of *Gladiator* Russell (useful bluffing value). Although Crowe M retired in 1996 aged 33 (due to severe knee problems), he was talking of making a comeback to the first-class game in 2011 at the age of 49. He was bluffing.

Perhaps, though, we shouldn't write him off yet. After all, WG Grace played Test cricket until the age of 50 (and he wasn't known to be the quickest between the wickets), and the great Yorkshire slow bowler Wilfred Rhodes played at international level when he was 52.

SOUTH AFRICA

Cricketing characteristics:

Batting: Take it in turn to carry the side: all of them from one to 11.

Bowling: Any shortcomings are compensated for by:

Fielding: Obsessively keen, awesomely good.

Debating point: When South Africa came out of the cricketing wilderness after the end of apartheid, the national team was soon under the leadership of an upstanding-looking chap called Hansie Cronje. He was young (captain at 24), clean cut, and seemed to have all the natural leadership qualities required of a nation seeking acceptance after the fall of a discredited regime.

Sadly, his Olympian appearance was a bluff. For rather than upholding high sporting ideals, Cronje accepted bribes to influence many of the games he took part in. He also tried to corrupt some of his teammates. When he finally admitted his wrongdoing, his excuse was that he had an 'unfortunate love of money.' In 2000, eight years after South Africa's readmission to international cricket, Cronje was banned from the professional game for life.

'Life' was unexpectedly short as he died in a plane crash in 2002. Two years later, he was voted the eleventh greatest South African of all time.

WEST INDIES

Cricketing characteristics:

Batting: Glorious. Uninhibited.

Bowling: Very fast. Beautiful to watch. Dreadful to face. In the 1970s and 1980s they had the most potent four-pronged fast-bowling attack in Test history led by Michael Holding and Malcolm Marshall. In the 1960s they had Wes Hall and Charlie Griffith. These names still strike terror into batsmen of all ages.

Fielding: Magnificent, unless they are losing (when they tend to lose interest).

Debating point: Having dominated world cricket from the mid 1970s to the early 1990s, the West Indies now look disorganised, unmotivated and generally off their game. What on earth went wrong? Many people blame the insidious cultural and sporting influence of the Americas, or athletics, or the joys of chillin'. On the other hand, given their victory in the 2012 Twenty20 World Cup, the 'Windies' might just be bluffing.

Once at the crease he removed his helmet and the bluff was revealed. It was noted that even the police and stewards joined in with the applause.

NOTABLE CRICKETING BLUFFS

The more high profile the bluffer, the more likely he or she is to be found out, as many politicians and celebrities have discovered (especially if they haven't previously armed themselves with the relevant *Bluffer's Guide*). And while we peripheral cricket bluffers usually only risk mild humiliation if exposed, those in the public eye could find themselves out of a job, or even in prison, if caught out exaggerating or lying. Cricket bluffing on a grand scale may exist for many reasons – some good, some bad. Often it involves concealing a weakness or pretending to be someone you're not. If you're bluffing for financial gain, shame on you and don't say you weren't warned.

BASIL D'OLIVEIRA

Here was a man who not only played brilliantly for Worcestershire and England but did much to reduce racial discrimination in sport. And yet the distinguished career of Basil D'Oliveira was based on a bluff.

Growing up, Dolly, as he came to be called, was one of the most gifted cricketers in South Africa. But because of his skin colour, he was banned from playing for his country. Racial segregation restricted him to playing on scrubbed matting pitches for non-white teams.

He had almost resigned himself to never playing top-class cricket when he got a last-minute offer from an English club in the Central Lancashire league. With the support of legendary cricket commentator John Arlott, he replaced West Indian bowler Wes Hall as the professional at amateur side Middleton.

After that, the next step was to play for a county side, but Dolly had a problem. In cricketing terms he was too old. In his autobiography, he admitted knocking years off his age (putting himself in his late 20s rather than mid-30s) when he made his debut for Worcestershire in 1964. Having bluffed his way into the county side, he played so well that two years later he was picked for England.

When he retired from the game in 1980, he suggested that he may in fact have been born in 1928. In which case he made his Worcestershire debut when he was 36, his England debut when he was 38, and played his last game as a professional when he was over 50. When he died in November 2011, his official date of birth was given as 1931. Only Dolly knew his real age.

Whatever the truth, the course of history may have been different if Dolly hadn't bluffed about his age. He would probably never have been picked for Worcestershire, let alone England. And if he hadn't been picked for England, there wouldn't have been the international row known as the D'Oliveira affair when, in 1968, the proposed England cricket tour of South Africa was cancelled because of his inclusion. And South Africa wouldn't have been thrown out of world sport, and apartheid might never...

Moral number one Bluffing can change the world (for the better).

ALLEN STANFORD

To be able to talk your way on to the hallowed turf of Lord's takes some doing under any circumstances. To land there in a helicopter with a glass chest full of banknotes and be sycophantically greeted by the game's top administrators is an outstanding bluff. Hats off, then, to Texan billionaire 'Sir' Allen Stanford who had proposed a Twenty20 series between England and an all-star West Indian side (which he rebranded the 'Stanford Superstars'). The prize money for the championship game exceeded $20 million – the largest sum ever offered for a single game in a cricket tournament.

The fact that Stanford was later stripped of his knighthood and imprisoned for defrauding thousands of investors in a $7 billion 'Ponzi' scheme was a bit of a setback but it didn't save the English cricket authorities' blushes.

In the event, only one match was played; England were thrashed by 10 wickets, making the West Indian players instant dollar millionaires. Stanford, who revelled in the publicity, was at one stage filmed with some of the England wives and girlfriends (WAGs). On a big screen at his Antigua ground, a picture flashed up of him vigorously bouncing Emily Prior (wife of England's wicketkeeper Matt) on his knee. Matt looked more than a little distracted as he crouched behind the stumps: his wife was heavily pregnant at the time.

Stanford was 62 before a lifetime of bluffing finally caught up with him. Up until then he'd done rather well. He made his first fortune in Texan real estate and then built a financial empire in the USA and Antigua where he paid for a cricket stadium and earned his honorary knighthood.

Before his trial, Stanford's lawyers claimed he was suffering from 'extensive retrograde amnesia'. In other words, he apparently couldn't remember a single thing.

Moral number two Bluffing that you have vast financial resources, when you don't, is very definitely not recommended. It is known as fraud.

KARL POWER

Many bluffers dream of walking out to play for England. In 2001, an unemployed labourer from Manchester with little knowledge of cricket (but a lot of bottle) did just that.

Earlier that year, Karl Power had pulled off his best-known stunt by appearing in Manchester United's team photo before the Champion's League game against Bayern Munich. He had bypassed the stadium security by bluffing that he was with a TV crew. Taking up his position with the rest of the lads in Munich's Olympic stadium was, he said, the best moment of his life. He then managed to slip back into the crowd and watched the match from the terraces.

His entry into the Test arena at Headingley didn't go

quite so smoothly.

Having locked himself in the gents, he was awaiting a call from an accomplice to tell him when the next wicket fell so he could walk out into the middle. Unfortunately, the next genuine batsman, Nasser Hussain, got there before him. Nevertheless, Power strolled out in helmet and full English regalia. Once at the crease he removed his helmet and the bluff was revealed. It was noted that even the police and stewards joined in the applause.

Power's bluffing career was far from over. Later, he managed to beat Michael Schumacher on to the winner's podium at the British Grand Prix and then managed a knock-up on Centre Court at Wimbledon before a Tim Henman match.

Moral number three Bluffers who have a laugh and do nobody any harm are generally quite popular.

MILES JUPP

Toddlers' pin-up Miles Jupp (Archie the Inventor in the children's BBC TV show *Balamory*) has the innocent look of a choirboy, perhaps because he once went to St George's School in Windsor which supplies choristers for The Queen. Jupp didn't quite make the chapel choir but he did later manage to rub shoulders with cricketing royalty. In 2006, he bluffed his way on to England's tour of India, wangling a press pass by saying he was reporting for BBC Radio Scotland and Welsh newspaper the *Western Mail*.

From a journalistic viewpoint the trip wasn't exactly a triumph. Radio Scotland refused to return his calls and when the only Welsh player was sent home, the *Western Mail* rapidly lost interest.

Stuck behind a pillar during the Second Test at Chandigarh, Jupp wondered why he'd 'travelled 4,000 miles to write for nobody about a thing I cannot see'.

On the plus side, he gathered some excellent material for a comedy tour and a book called *Fibber in the Heat.*

Moral number four Bluffing doesn't always work out quite as you might have hoped.

CRICKET IN LITERATURE

The close links between cricket and literature may help to extricate you from a tight spot. A quick change of subject may be advisable for those who find themselves out of their cricketing depth, and a nodding acquaintance with the connections of some writers to the game might provide the necessary life raft.

The creator of Jeeves and Bertie Wooster, PG Wodehouse, could be described as the patron saint of cricketing bluffers. 'A man may be an excellent sportsman in theory,' he wrote, 'even if he fail in practice.' Quite so.

In a book called *Beyond a Boundary*, the Trinidadian writer CLR James unhelpfully coined a more dispiriting aphorism: 'What do they know of cricket who only cricket know?' Don't worry about what this means. Simply say wistfully that *Beyond a Boundary* is the seminal work on cricket.

What is crucial is that you should exploit any overlaps that might exist between your particular areas of knowledge (politics, literature, tropical fish, whatever) and, by definition, your limited grasp of cricket. That's the key to becoming an all-round cricketing bluffer – with a safety net.

Luckily, literature is full of handy cross references. Some famous novelists like Charles Dickens and Anthony Trollope have included cricketing scenes in their books. Other, usually lesser, writers have produced fiction entirely devoted to the game. Hugh de Selincourt's *The Cricket Match* and AG Macdonell's *England, Their England* are useful examples. More useful to bluffers are wordsmiths who had a crack at the game themselves. You might well impress someone by knowing which Nobel Prize winner played first-class cricket (not Jeffrey Archer) and which writer of detective fiction took the wicket of WG Grace. Here, then, are some names to conjure with.

JM BARRIE

He might have created Peter Pan but his real passion was cricket. Sadly, he was pretty hopeless at it. A contemporary described JM Barrie as 'small [he was 5ft 3in], frail…and there was nothing athletic about his appearance'. That, as all bluffers will know, is not necessarily a handicap. To his credit, he not only stuck at the game but put together his own team – Allahakbarries Cricket Club. It was mainly composed of other literary coves including the creators of the *Father Brown* stories (GK Chesterton), *The History of Mr Polly* (HG Wells), *Winnie-the-Pooh* (AA Milne) and *Three Men in a Boat* (Jerome K Jerome).

To be fair, they never claimed to be much good. They called themselves the Allahakbarries because Barrie thought Allahakbar meant 'Heaven help us' in Arabic. (A more accurate translation would be 'God is great'.) On the way to their first game, one of their number confessed that he didn't know which side of the bat was used to strike the ball (obviously not a bluffer). Unsurprisingly, they were thrashed by their opponents – the village team at Shere in Surrey. Nevertheless, the Allahakbarries carried gamely on through many Edwardian summers, almost up to the outbreak of the First World War.

He might have created
Peter Pan but his real passion was cricket.
Sadly, he was pretty hopeless at it.

SIR ARTHUR CONAN DOYLE

In contrast to JM Barrie, Doyle was an all-round sportsman. A strapping six-footer, he kept goal for Portsmouth FC, captained Crowborough Beacon Golf Club, pioneered skiing in Switzerland and played 10 first-class games for the MCC. His bowling was slow and described as of 'puzzling flight'; so puzzling, in fact, that in 1899 he took seven for 61 for the MCC against Cambridgeshire at Lord's. He was also a hard-hitting batsman; in 1902 he scored 32 not out against Leicestershire and made a top first-class score of 43 against London County.

His crowning glory came in 1900 when he captured the wicket of WG Grace in a first-class match. The great man, playing for London County, was 52 and had scored 110 to notch up his 1,000 runs for the season. Perhaps, though, it was Doyle's puzzling flight which fooled him into hitting a top edge which was caught behind. Doyle was in seventh heaven and proceeded to write an extremely long poem about it. Who can blame him?

Doyle is best known, of course, for creating Sherlock Holmes, whose name, apparently, was inspired by two Nottinghamshire cricketers: Mordecai Sherwin and Frank Shacklock.

PG WODEHOUSE

As a player, observer and passionate fan, Wodehouse had a thorough grasp of all the nuances of cricket. At Dulwich College he was an accomplished fast bowler but he once concluded in an essay on the game that 'it is, on the whole, better to be a cricket spectator rather than a cricket player. No game affords the spectator such unique opportunities of exerting his critical talents.' Spot on, old boy!

While many of his readers would consider Jeeves and Wooster his finest creations, Wodehouse apparently told George Orwell that he thought his best work was a public school cricket story, *Mike.*

As a new boy facing the school's best bowler in the nets, Mike Jackson is asked whether he's in a panic. Wodehouse writes: 'The fact was that he had far too good an opinion of himself to be nervous. An entirely modest person seldom makes a good batsman. Batting is one of those things which demands first and foremost a thorough belief in oneself.'

His novels featuring Psmith are equally perceptive. In *Psmith in the City* Wodehouse describes a country house game during which a bank manager commits the cardinal crime of walking in front of the sight screen as a player is on the verge of a century. Few things are more frowned on in cricket apart from, as previously discussed, accepting a bribe.

In his younger days Wodehouse occasionally stiffened the attack of the Allahakbarries with his right-arm, fast-medium bowling. Later, when he had given up playing and emigrated to the USA, he confessed to missing the game more than any other aspect of English life.

SAMUEL BECKETT

'Hanging around for something to happen' might be a description of watching a dull passage of play in a cricket match or of any passage in Samuel Beckett's best-known play. *Waiting for Godot* helped the Irish writer win the Nobel Prize and confirmed him as one of the most important literary figures of the twentieth century. What is less well known is his aptitude with bat and ball.

In his youth Beckett was a gritty (his own description) left-handed opening bat and a medium-pace, left-arm bowler. He played two first-class games for Dublin University against Northamptonshire, thus becoming the only Nobel laureate with an entry in *Wisden*. Looking at his figures, literature didn't rob cricket of a brightly burning star. He averaged a meagre 8.75 with the bat and bowled 23 wicketless overs for 64 runs.

At the age of 22 Beckett settled in Paris where cricketing opportunities were scarce. He did, however, manage to get almost fatally stabbed when he was attacked by a madman in the street. Nothing so exciting happens in *Waiting for Godot.*

HAROLD PINTER

The rhythm of Harold Pinter's plays, with their long pauses and occasional bursts of action, has also been compared to the game of cricket. Like Beckett, Pinter was a Nobel laureate who mined the absurdities of the human condition and was mustard-keen on the game. Although Pinter didn't play at first-class level, he was associated for many years with the 'Gaieties' – a club for players of a theatrical persuasion. He also came up with an entertaining quote about cricket: 'I tend to believe that cricket is the greatest thing that God ever created on earth. Certainly greater than sex, although sex isn't too bad either.' This might have been something he didn't share with his wife, Lady Antonia Fraser.

The cast of one of his plays, *No Man's Land,* includes characters named after former players. There's Hirst (George Hirst, Yorkshire all-rounder), Briggs (Johnny Briggs, Lancashire slow bowler) and Spooner (RH Spooner, Lancashire batsman).

Pinter's hero, though, was the great Yorkshire opening batsman Len Hutton whom he first saw as a boy when he was an evacuee in Leeds. Hutton's bat, he recalled, seemed 'an extension of his nervous system'.

Pinter also wrote a number of screenplays which feature cricket, including *Accident* (starring Michael York and Dirk Bogarde) and *The Go-Between* – his adaptation of the LP Hartley novel which opens with the words: 'The past is a foreign country; they do things differently there.' The same could be said of cricket. Pinter did much of his writing in a room full of cricket memorabilia, including a full set of *Wisdens* (about 150 volumes).

SIMON RAVEN

At Charterhouse school, Simon Raven played in the same team as Peter May who became one of England's finest batsmen. Unlike May, Raven was a bit of a bounder with, as someone once said, 'the mind of a cad and the pen of an angel'. He wove cricket into fiction more convincingly than most other twentieth-century writers. In an early novel called *Close of Play,* the on-field action is integral to the plot. It concerns a dissolute young man called Hugo Warren, taken under the wing of a kindly prep school headmaster and former Kent county cricketer after his parents' death. When the school falls into financial trouble, Hugo reneges on a promise to help in favour of alcohol, sex and cricket. What a frightful cad. In the course of a match he even manages to kill his cousin by striking him with a vicious pull shot. When, eventually, the failing prep school is sold to make way for a council estate, a last game is played before the bulldozers move in and Hugo has a memorable final stand with his mentor before being drowned in the swimming pool by friends disgusted by his selfish behaviour. That's cricketers for you – driven by a sense of fair play and an unerring need to do the right thing.

Another of this neglected writer's books, an autobiography called *Shadows on the Grass,* earned the distinction of being described by cricket writer EW Swanton as 'the filthiest book on cricket', a title which it is safe to assume is not often contested.

At his best Raven captures the joy, brutality and subtlety of cricket in a vivid present tense. As for his caddishness, at least it was usually witty. When he received a telegram from the mother of his child saying, 'Wife and baby starving send money soonest,' he sent the following reply: 'Sorry no money suggest eat baby.'

THE HISTORICAL CONTEXT

The important thing to remember is that the whole of cricket is history, most of it intricate and unimportant, much of it ill-recorded and unmemorable – what more could an honest bluffer ask for? While the more adventurous among you might like to flirt with the present or recent past, those of a more conservative disposition might feel safer bluffing about a period few can remember. The further back you go, the less likely you are to be contradicted. So this chapter doesn't go beyond the Second World War.

Memorise some of the following and you'll be more than halfway to being the scourge of every pavilion, Long Room and bar from here to the MCG (the familiar way of referring to the Melbourne Cricket Ground).

1666 First reference to a cricket club – St Albans.

1709 First county match – Kent v Surrey.

1774 First Laws of Cricket are drafted. Some nobs and gents met in the Star and Garter, Pall Mall, and drafted laws that still cover the basic game today. Before falling to the floor, awash with claret, they drew up rules covering the size of bat, weight of ball, number of stumps, how dismissals could occur, duties of umpires, etc. They also attempted to regulate betting, which was prodigious on cricket matches – and everything else; in 1757 you could get four-to-one on George II being killed in battle. Their one law that has not survived was that visiting teams could choose the location of the pitch.

1782 White Conduit Club (WCC), gents only, one of the forerunners of the MCC, is formed.

1787 The WCC becomes the MCC (Marylebone Cricket Club), by turning its first initial upside-down.

1787 Thomas Lord (of Lord's fame) built his first cricket ground in Dorset Square.

1789 First English tour planned. Unfortunately the destination was Paris, and the tour was cancelled when the French Revolution broke out. It seems typical of the French to get their priorities so absurdly wrong.

1811 Thomas Lord opened his second cricket ground, the lease on the first having expired.

1813 Parliament decided to cut a canal through Lord's second cricket ground. Lord moved it to St John's Wood, where Lord's has remained.

1836 First county club formed – Sussex ground.

1844 First international match – Canada v USA.

1859 First overseas tour. An English team visited Canada and the USA. The Americans very sensibly postponed their Civil War for two years to allow this tour to proceed.

1861 First English tour of Australia. This included a single-wicket match (*see* 'Glossary', page 114) between Mr Griffith and 11 assorted Aussies. The Aussies failed to make a single run between them and then bowled a wide at Mr Griffith, thus immediately losing the match. It is best to keep quiet about this late on a Saturday night in Shepherd's Bush or any other part of Australia.

1864 Overarm bowling legalised. Until then, bowling had been 'under' or 'round' arm. Women were the first to stop bowling underarm as they nearly broke their wrists on their crinolines.

1877 First Test match – Australia v England.

THE GOLDEN AGES

Cricket has had several Golden Ages and each one would seem to precede a major war, so let's hope that there will be no more. In the early days, cricket matches were ramshackle affairs with bizarre scratch sides: Middlesex with Two of Berkshire and One of Kent v Essex with Two More Given; Five of the Globe Club v Four of the MCC; The Original English Lady Cricketers, elegantly and appropriately attired v Similar; Twenty-Three ofKent v Thirteen of England; and A One-Legged XI v A One-

Armed XI – of which it was reported:

> *The men with one leg beat the one-arms by one hundred and three runnings. After the match was finished, the eleven one-legged men ran one hundred yards for twenty guineas. The three first divided the money.*

FIRST GOLDEN AGE (1848-1882)

Bathed in a sea of nostalgia, the First Golden Age is captured in poetry. It was the time of Henry Newbolt's:

> 'There's a breathless hush in the Close tonight…'

and Francis Thompson's:

> 'For the field is full of shades as I near the shadowy coast,
> And a ghostly batsman plays to the bowling of a ghost…'

Like all Golden Ages, it was a time of great batsmen, but was brought to an end by a 'Demon Bowler' – the mighty Australian Frederick Spofforth.

In 1882, Spofforth wrecked Grace's MCC side at Lord's, taking six wickets for four runs in 23 balls, and then 'killed' English cricket at the Oval. England only needed 34 runs to win, with eight wickets left (including that of Grace), when Spofforth is reported to have said: 'Boys, this thing can be done.' He promptly took seven wickets and Australia won by seven runs. There followed agrarian outrages in Ireland, war in Egypt and the Sudan, riots in Burma, the collapse of Gladstone's government and the end of the First Golden Age.

SECOND GOLDEN AGE (1899-1914)

A plethora of great batsmen: Hobbs, Hayward, Abel, MacLaren, Ranji, Trumper, Armstrong and Wilfred Rhodes. CB Fry was regarded as the most glamorous figure of the Second Golden Age until a jolly unsporting biography revealed what he was up to besides playing cricket and football for England, going as a delegate to the League of Nations, breaking the world long jump record and being invited to be King of Albania.

Then there was Gilbert 'the Croucher' Jessop, who scored two of the fastest centuries ever (perhaps the fastest ever when it is taken into account that hits over the ropes counted as only four runs in Jessop's time); Frank Woolley (reckoned the most graceful cricketer ever); Albert Trott (the only man to hit a ball over the pavilion at Lord's); and the Hon FS Jackson (who managed to play cricket with his sleeves rolled down but not buttoned at the wrist).

There were also a few great and long-suffering bowlers. The best of them, Tom Richardson, who bowled fast all day at the Oval, would pack his bag at close of play and walk 12 miles home, stopping, it is said, at every pub along the way.

By 1914, Spofforth was 61 and too old to demolish the Second Golden Age, so the Kaiser (right-hand cowshot bat and poor close-to-wicket fielder) intervened instead.

THIRD GOLDEN AGE (1930-1939)

This was again a time of long hot summers, easy wickets and great batsmen. Far more triple centuries were scored in the 1930s than in any other decade. Among the giants were Bradman, Sutcliffe, Hammond, McCabe, Headley, Ponsford, Duleepsinhji (Ranji's nephew) and a very young Hutton. There were also a few who hung on from the Second Golden Age. Among them were Woolley, Hobbs and, lastly, Rhodes who, at the age of 52, bowled 45 overs for 39 runs against the West Indies, a feat unlikely to be repeated.

The Third Golden Age came to an end on 1 September 1939, when Hedley Verity took seven wickets for nine runs in six overs at Hove – and Hitler (who never played the game) invaded Poland.

FAMOUS CRICKETERS

The exploits of Bradman, Hobbs, Hammond, Botham, Bedser, Sobers, Sutcliffe, Ranjitsinhji, Kapil Dev, Imran, Lindwall, Fry, Grace, Gunn, Verity, etc. are all to be found in dozens of books about cricket. Most of them have already been the subject of several biographies. The thing to do, therefore, is to have your own list of cricketers who were famous once upon a time, but who are hardly ever discussed today. You can blithely use any of the following:

'LUMPY' STEVENS (1735-1819)

Herts, Kent and All England. A demon bowler, employed as a gardener by the fourth Earl of Sandwich (the cheese-and-pickle one), who appointed many great cricketers to his staff. Lumpy bowled fast and dangerously, downhill wherever possible – in those days the winner of the toss could choose the lie of the pitch. His worst afternoon was in 1775. Five Men of Kent needed one more wicket to beat Five Men of Hambledon. Several times Lumpy bowled 'through' the wicket, for those were the days of only two stumps. Lumpy's language is not recorded in *Wisden*.

JOHN SMALL (1737-1826)

Hants and All England. The happy batsman who was at the crease when poor Lumpy was bowling that May afternoon in 1775. Small was a cheerful man who hung a sign outside his door which said:

Here lives John Small,
Makes bat and ball,
Pitches a wicket, plays at cricket
With any man in England.

You don't see signs like that nowadays.

DAVID HARRIS OF HAMBLEDON (1755-1803)

Poor fielder, much handicapped by gout. Had to sit in a large armchair on field to rest after each ball was bowled.

SHOCK WHITE (MID-EIGHTEENTH CENTURY; EXACT DATES UNKNOWN)

Famous for turning up one afternoon in Reigate, back in the 1770s, with a bat that was wider than the wicket. A good wheeze, but like most brilliant inventions it was immediately outlawed by a law specifically aimed to do so.

GEORGE BROWN OF BRIGHTON (1783-1857)

Sussex and England. Bowled underarm so fast that he killed a dog on the boundary.

F WILLIAM 'NONPAREIL' LILLYWHITE (1792-1854)

Sussex. Father of Fred Jnr who founded Lillywhites, the famous sports store on Piccadilly Circus. In 1831, he broke the record for the number of wickets taken in a season. One of the first round-arm bowlers. Once took 14 wickets for South v North, but that was in an age when they sometimes played about 120 a side. He was still playing at 60, although he had to be carried to the wicket to bat.

MASTER LUDD (NINETEENTH CENTURY; EXACT DATES UNKNOWN)

A pragmatic cricketer, once struck on the foot by John Jackson of Notts. Ludd hobbled in agony. Jackson screamed his appeal. 'Not out,' said the umpire. 'Mebbe not,' said Master Ludd, 'but I'm a-goin'.' And he limped away, presumably to continue his other career as a machine wrecker in factories.

FULLER PILCH (1804-1870)

Norfolk and Kent. A professional in the days when professionals earned very little, and usually had another occupation. He was a tailor. Pilch was a 'most famous player' who scored more runs than anyone else in cricket until WG Grace came along. To help him in this, and to make pitches play truer and faster, Pilch took his own scythe along and recut the grass before he batted.

ALFRED MYNN (1807-1861)

Kent and All England. Like Pilch, Mynn was an impecunious professional, a hop merchant who occasionally went to prison for his inability to pay his creditors. Top-hatted, six foot one, 20 stone but graceful (so they say) in every movement. The first really great round-arm fast bowler – so fast that opponents used specially heavy bats against him, more for protection than to score runs. Known as the 'Lion of Kent', Mynn was an all-rounder who opened the batting as well as the bowling and became single-wicket champion of All England in 1846, when he beat a violinist by an innings. Ten years earlier he had nearly lost a leg, severely damaged during a long innings – they did not wear pads in those days. Being too large for an inside seat, Mynn was strapped to the top of a stagecoach and carried all the way from Leicester to a surgeon in London, who, fortunately, decided against amputation.

SIR C AUBREY 'ROUND THE CORNER' SMITH (1863-1948)

Cambridge University, Sussex, Transvaal and England. The nickname derived from his odd and angular run-up to the wicket when bowling. Captained England in his only Test in South Africa in 1888. Did well. Subsequently moved to Hollywood and became a movie actor. In this capacity he was about as good as you would expect most fast-medium bowlers to be.

GH SIMPSON-HAYWARD (1871-1936)

Worcestershire and England. The last great underarm 'lob' bowler. In 1909 he captained an MCC team on a tour of Egypt, usually bowling his lobs with the blazing desert sun behind him. Most of his opponents retired blind.

There's no point in pretending that you know everything about cricket – nobody does – but if you've got this far and you've absorbed at least a modicum of the information and advice contained within these pages, then you will almost certainly know more than 99% of the rest of the human race about what cricket is, how it is played, who plays it, what the point of it is, and why a match can last for up to five days with breaks for lunch, tea and, of course, rain.

What you now do with this information is up to you, but here's a suggestion: be confident about your new-found knowledge, see how far it takes you, but above all have fun using it. You are now a bona fide expert in the art of bluffing about the world's most puzzling and incomprehensible game.

Think you're ready to shine with your knowledge of cricket? Test it first with our quiz at bluffers.com.

GLOSSARY

Bails The two cylindrical bits of wood that sit atop the three stumps. They have to be knocked off for someone to be 'out'. If they remain firmly on the stumps then the batsman is not out. Not that any bluffer should ever condone cheating, but it might be a good idea to carry a tube of superglue when at the crease.

Ball-tampering Making the ball too shiny by applying unguents, or too rough by picking at the seam or rubbing mud on it. It is cricket's equivalent of not standing for the National Anthem; it just isn't done.

Beamer A fast, potentially lethal ball that flies straight at the batsman's head. Bowlers always pretend that they didn't mean to.

Benefit A reward given to old lags who have performed faithfully for their club. Fundraising activities include special 'celebrity' matches with showbiz XIs, dinner dances and collection boxes passed round grounds. The poor old lag then has to justify the money that has been collected.

Bouncer/Bumper A fast, potentially lethal ball that bounces just in front of the bowler and then rises towards the batsman's head. Bowlers always pretend that they did mean to.

Box A metal or plastic codpiece worn by all batsmen, nervous fielders and forgetful bowlers.

Cover/Off side That side of the field that your nose points to when batting.

Cowshot A scything blow that has little chance of making contact, but is very exciting if it does. The name has a scathing, rural connotation.

Cut A sophisticated attempt to hit the ball once it is past you but before it has reached the wicketkeeper's hands, otherwise there is the terrible noise of knuckles splintering.

Declaration A means by which the batting side bring their innings to a premature close, showing off and hinting that they have already scored more runs than they will need.

Dolly Supposedly a very easy catch. Anyone who has ever played cricket will tell you that there is no such thing.

Duckworth Lewis Method Not a form of birth control but an impossibly complicated, yet reliable, formula to revise a batting target in a rain-affected one-day game. That's the majority of them.

Follow-on A means by which the fielding side shows off, making their opponents bat again because they have scored so few runs.

Full toss ('full bunger') A ball that fails to bounce before it reaches the batsman. Very easy to hit, therefore, since it is not subject to the vagaries of the pitch or the wiles of the bowler's spin. Usually ends up in the Squire's duck pond.

Half-volley Military salute fired by an army too poor to afford enough rounds of ammunition. Also a ball that lands just in front of the batsman.

Hoick Noise made by a cricketer about to expectorate. Also cowshot.

In A word you do not shout when you reach the safety of the other end of the pitch having made a run.

Jaffa An unplayable ball with an erratic and unpredictable flight. It usually surprises the bowler more than the batsman because it is generally a complete fluke.

Leg/On side That side of the field your bum points to when you are batting.

Leg break A ball that starts on your bum side then heads towards the off side.

Long hop A ball that lands appetisingly way in front of the batsman, giving him plenty of time to roll up his sleeves, spit on his hands (*see* 'Hoick') and tonk it to the boundary.

Made a run A phrase you never use. The correct description is 'scored a run'.

Maiden Six balls in succession by the same bowler without a run being scored, i.e., a phenomenon without blemish.

Nightwatchman Poor sod of a batsman who is sent in late at night – when the light is bad, wickets are falling and the bowler and fielders are rampant with success – to protect much better batsmen. Some of us feel that our whole way of life is founded on similar principles.

Notts Trots (also Surrey Hurries and Delhi Belly) Uproariously humorous term given by cricketers to the runs that have nothing to do with cricket.

Off break A ball that starts on your nose side and turns to hit you in the box.

Out A word you do not shout when one of the other side is dismissed.

Over-rate a) The number of overs bowled in an hour; or b) what the press do to any young English cricketer who scores more than 10 against Australia or the West Indies.

Playing with a straight bat One of many cricket phrases that have leaked into general use. Means conforming to accepted behaviour or not taking unnecessary risks. Hitting the ball with a horizontal bat is considered far more risky.

Pull Hitting a ball from the nose to the bum side.

Seam The part of the cricket ball where they sew it together.

Seam bowling The ball is deliberately bowled onto its

seam to cause random deviation when it hits the pitch.

Selectors Formerly a group of toffs who chose the England team. Now more likely to be swanky ex-pros.

Sighters A term that seeks to excuse bowling a load of tripe that goes in all directions save at the stumps.

Sight screen White painted boards, often on little wheels, which are placed on the boundary behind the bowler's arm so that members in the pavilion cannot see what is going on, i.e., the cricket is screened from their sight.

Single-wicket cricket Ancient form of the game recently revived. A sort of gladiatorial contest where one-person teams compete for prize money, usually in a park in Hong Kong.

Surrey Cut Name given to a flashing and flamboyant stroke that seeks to send the ball nose side, but instead snicks it between the batsman's legs to the bum side. Often profitable but never graceful.

Taverner Name given to someone too poor or too yobbish to be a full member of a cricket club but who has alcoholic aspirations.

Tonk A mighty and primitive blow at the ball.

Yorker A ball that pitches either a) on your foot, severely injuring and/or dismissing you lbw; or b) just underneath your bat, squeezing through and bowling you; or c) right on the bottom of your bat, sending shockwaves up and down both arms and giving you the feeling that you have spent the last six hours wrestling with a pneumatic drill. Called 'Yorker' because a Lancashire player was the first to master the skill.

BLUFFING NOTES

Bluffing Notes

Bluffing Notes

Bluffing Notes

Bluffing Notes

Bluffing Notes

Bluffing Notes

Bluffing Notes

Bluffing Notes

Bluffing Notes